PRAISE FOR *CHASTITY*

"This book is a welcome additio~~n~~
seeking to clarify a stronger and m~~o~~
between our sexuality and our spir~~it~~
how chastity got such a bad rap but I am grateful Fr. Ron
has initiated the work of reclaiming it as an attitude and
a practice that fosters a spirituality *wholesome enough* to
celebrate sexuality as a beautiful gift from God intended
to be linked to exuberance, spirituality and delight.
What a blessing!"

—RUTH HALEY BARTON, Founder, Transforming Center,
and author of *Sacred Rhythms*

"Fr. Ron Rolheiser, in this daring and holy book, defines
sexual longing in the context of love and patient reserve as
we seek within ourselves what is truly meant by the chastity
of our souls in the presence of those we love. This is a book
for young people seeking a way to the marriage bed, and a
celebration for those who have already discovered in
their relationships the meaning of commitment,
compassion, sexual joy, and spiritual ecstasy."

—CHRISTOPHER DE VINCK, author of *Things That Matter Most:
Essays on Home, Friendship, and Love*

"It takes both courage and a very clear head for a Catholic
theologian to take on any issue regarding sexuality today.
Ron Rolheiser succeeds here in a very positive, honest,
and helpful way! His approach is brilliantly not
sin-centered but value-centered. Bravo!"

—RICHARD ROHR, O.F.M.

"Ron Rolheiser has a rare gift of discerning and expressing the deepest movements of our souls. In this courageous and prophetic book he presents chastity – defined as respect, reverence and patience – as the pathway to joy and the fullness of life. In one way or another you'll hear your own story told as you read this book, and you'll experience yourself as being wisely and compassionately guided to your heart's home."

—MICHELLE JONES, author of *The Gospel Mysticism of Ruth Burrows: Going to God with Empty Hands*

"Ronald Rolheiser's new book offers a rich, beautifully written and reflective reinterpretation of the theme of 'chastity.' He expresses his spiritual vision through insightful images that present an honest way forward accessible to all of us. He asks us in challenging ways to radically rethink how we conventionally understand the word 'chastity' and limit its scope to a narrow view of sexuality. Ronald Rolheiser's alternative perspective promotes 'healthy' chastity in all our lives as a value that focuses on proper reverence and respect for other people. This includes sexuality as a way of affirming other people rather than exploiting them."

—PHILIP SHELDRAKE, Professor, Senior Fellow, and Research Director, Institute for the Study of Contemporary Spirituality at Oblate School of Theology

Chastity
and the
Soul

You Are Holy Ground

Ronald Rolheiser

PARACLETE PRESS
Brewster, Massachusetts

To my mother and father, George and Mathilda Rolheiser,
who modeled a healthy chastity.

———————————————

2024 First Printing

Chastity and the Soul: You Are Holy Ground
Copyright © 2024 by Ronald Rolheiser
ISBN 978-1-64060-947-1

Scripture quotations marked (NRSVCE) are taken from the New Revised Standard Version Updated Edition. Copyright © 2021 National Council of Churches of Christ in the United States of America. Used by permission. All rights reserved worldwide.

Scripture quotations marked (NLT) are taken from the Holy Bible, New Living Translation, copyright ©1996, 2004, 2015 by Tyndale House Foundation. Used by permission of Tyndale House Publishers, Carol Stream, Illinois 60188. All rights reserved.

The Paraclete Press name and logo (dove on cross) are trademarks of Paraclete Press.

   Library of Congress Cataloging-in-Publication Data
Names: Rolheiser, Ronald, author.
Title: Chastity and the soul : you are holy ground / Ronald Rolheiser.
Description: Brewster, Massachusetts : Paraclete Press, 2024. | Summary:
   "Rolheiser champions the notion of chastity in its fullest meaning:
   respect, patience, reverence, and a God-given gift of propriety in every
   area of life-not just in the area of sex"-- Provided by publisher.
Identifiers: LCCN 2023045571 (print) | LCCN 2023045572 (ebook) | ISBN
   9781640609471 | ISBN 9781640609488 (epub)
Subjects: LCSH: Chastity. | Christian life. | BISAC: RELIGION / Christian
   Living / Personal Growth | RELIGION / Christian Living / Social Issues
Classification: LCC BJ1533.C4 .R654 2024 (print) | LCC BJ1533.C4 (ebook)
   | DDC 241/.664--dc23/eng/20231130
LC record available at https://lccn.loc.gov/2023045571
LC ebook record available at https://lccn.loc.gov/2023045572

10 9 8 7 6 5 4 3 2 1

Published by Paraclete Press
Brewster, Massachusetts
www.paracletepress.com

Printed in the United States of America

CONTENTS

PREFACE

*C*an purity be a word that is ever used without a cringe?" Lisbeth During asks this question at the end of her book, *The Chastity Plot*, though she asks it as a sincere probe, not as a cynical judgment on those who still defend sexual purity. The same question might be asked about the word *chastity*, one of the long-time guardians of purity. Can the word be used without a cringe? The concept of chastity has fallen on hard times.

Several years ago, I was invited to speak to a group of students at a Catholic university. The invitation came with a request and a caveat. I was to speak on chastity, but ideally, I was to avoid using the word. The Dean of Theology, who had invited me, had appraised the situation this way: perhaps more than anything else, the students need a challenge to chastity, but they are so turned off by the word that if we mention it in the title, very few will show up.

His hunch was right on both scores: the need for chastity in their lives and their aversion to the word. That's also true for our culture.

For many today, the word chastity has negative connotations. Outside of a constantly shrinking number of select church circles, the word *chastity* sets off mostly negative alarms. Within our highly secularized and sophisticated world, for the most part chastity is identified with naïveté, sexual timidity, religious fundamentalism, a toxic overemphasis on sexual purity, a lack of sophistication, and something that made more sense in another age. Commonly, the notion is ridiculed, even in some religious circles. Very few people today dare talk about saving sex for marriage or about chastity as virtue.

What's behind this? Why this negativity and disdain toward chastity?

Partly this is based on a number of popular perceptions. Chastity is often seen as grounded in a religious fundamentalism, which our culture today either disdains or pities (*"Chastity for Jesus"*). As well, the notion of chastity is seen as a product of the Roman Catholic church's long-standing, one-sided emphasis on virginity and celibacy and its failure to articulate a healthy, robust spirituality of sex. It's hard to argue with perceptions, except to say that the reasons for the demise of the concept of chastity in our culture are much more complex than this.

Admittedly, the church's catechesis about chastity is part of the problem. My suspicion is that a good number of people are negative vis-à-vis the notion because of how the concept has been presented to them. Our churches and moral teachers have to assume some of the blame and admit that far too often the concept of chastity has been presented, however unintentionally, precisely as a naïveté, a repression, and as an overemphasis on sexual purity. There's a parallel here to how atheism finds its ground. Just as so much atheism is a parasite feeding off bad religion, so too much of the negativity towards the concept of chastity is a parasite feeding off unhealthy religious teaching.

However, our culture's negativity toward the notion of chastity feeds off more than a less-than-healthy catechesis. The culprit? Sophistication as a virtue that is an end in itself. In short, our culture prizes personal sophistication above most everything else, and when sophistication is so highly prized, chastity easily looks like naïveté and ignorance. Is it?

At the end of the day, is chastity a sexual repression, an unhealthy timidity, a toxic overemphasis on sexual purity, a religious fundamentalism, a pitiable pre-sophistication? Admittedly, that can sometimes be the case. However, there's a strong case too for chastity.

In 2013, Donna Freitas, the author of a number of books on sexuality and consent, published a study entitled *The End of Sex: How Hookup Culture is Leaving a Generation Unhappy, Sexually Unfulfilled, and Confused about Intimacy.* That title is the book in caption. Nowhere in the book (and for this she has been unjustly criticized by some church groups) does she ever say that what is happening in our culture today in terms of soulless sex is wrong or sinful. She doesn't have to. She simply spells out the consequences—unhappiness, confusion, sexual depression.

A generation earlier, the renowned educator Allan Bloom, writing from a purely secular perspective, came to the same conclusion. Looking at the bright, highly sophisticated young students he was teaching, he concluded that the very unbridled sophistication they so prided themselves in (which he termed "the absence of chastity in their lives") had this effect in their lives: it left them "erotically lame."

And so, I suggest that chastity merits another look. There's childishness and there's childlikeness. There's hook-up sex and there's soul-sex. There's religious fundamentalism and there's the wisdom of divine revelation. There's the overemphasis on sexual purity and there's the dehumanizing disrespect for others (that the *#MeToo* movement is standing up to). There's a certain ennui and fatigue in an ultra-sophistication that believes all taboos may be broken, and there's a vibrancy and happiness that's felt in keeping your shoes off before the burning bush. In every one of these dualisms, chastity speaks for soul, for wisdom, for respect, and for happiness.

This book will elaborate on this, namely, the death of chastity in our culture, the negative consequences of that on our souls and in our lives, the need for a healthy chastity in our lives, what constitutes that healthy chastity, and the positive consequences that this can have in our lives—so that we can say the word *chastity* without a cringe.

PART ONE

Chastity as Proper Reverence, Respect, and Patience

"Do not come any closer," God said. "Take off your sandals, for the place where you are standing is holy ground."

—*Exodus 3:5,* NLT

CHAPTER 1

What is Chastity?

The notion of chastity has fallen on hard times today, both in our culture and often also inside our churches. It is associated either with a certain childish naïveté (like believing in Santa and the Easter Bunny, nice for the kids) or with sexual repression. It is more mocked than admired. Sadly, this is based on a misunderstanding, and equally sad are the consequences we pay for this.

What is chastity? Chastity is about proper reverence in every area of life, not just in the area of sex. In his book *Zorba the Greek*, Nikos Kazantzakis shares this story: He had been watching a moth come out of its cocoon. The process was fascinating but painstakingly slow. After watching this interminably slow metamorphosis, he eventually lost patience and applied some heat to the moth. It sped up the process, and the moth emerged more quickly. . . . But because the process had been pressured to come to its culmination earlier than nature intended, the moth emerged with damaged wings. It could not fly.

That is a poignant image for chastity. Chastity is not first of all about premature or illicit sex. At its root, it is not primarily even a sexual concept, though given the power and urgency of sex, faults in chastity often are within the area of sexuality. Chastity is about the way we experience, about the appropriateness and maturity of any experience, sex included.

In essence, chastity is *proper reverence, respect,* and *patience.* And, in a culture that is often characterized by irreverence, disrespect, and impatience, it is much needed. To be chaste is to experience people, things, places, entertainment, the phases of life, life's opportunities, and sex, in a way that does not violate them or us. In brief, I am chaste when I relate to others in a way that does not violate their moral, psychological, emotional, sexual, or aesthetic contours. I am chaste when I do not let irreverence or impatience denigrate or cheapen what is gift, and when I let life, others, and sex, unfold according to their own proper dictates.

Conversely, I lack chastity when I transgress boundaries prematurely or irreverently, when I violate anything so as to somehow not respect its full integrity. Chastity is respect, patience, and reverence, and the fruits of that are integration, gratitude, and joy. Lack of chastity is disrespect, impatience, and irreverence, and the fruits of chastity are disintegration, bitterness, and cynicism (all infallible signs of the lack of chastity). Chastity is reverence and, in the end, all sin is irreverence.

In a sense (and I submit this is not an overstatement) chastity is the key to everything. Joy, community, love, and even full enjoyment of sex depend upon chastity. When a society is chaste, community will happen; when a family is chaste, it will find joy in its everyday life; when lovers are chaste, they will experience a deeper ecstasy in sex; when a church is chaste, it will radiate the fruits of the Spirit. The reverse is also true. Chaos, joylessness, erotic numbness, and hardness of heart are generally faults in one's chastity.

Scripture provides us with a very powerful metaphor for chastity. In the call of Moses, we see him drawn to the fire of a burning bush, and as he approaches the bush, God says to him: *Take off your shoes, because the ground you are standing on is holy*. Every person we stand before is holy ground. Life is holy ground. Sex is holy ground. Having our shoes off is a metaphor for reverence, respect, and patience—for chastity.

A generation ago, before the sexual revolution, Albert Camus wrote: "Chastity alone is connected with personal progress. There is a time when moving beyond it is a victory—when it is released from its moral imperatives. But this quickly turns to defeat afterwards."

What is meant by those words? Whatever they mean, they are not understood by our generation, which considers the move beyond chastity as anything but a defeat. For our generation, this is progress, a sophistication, a liberation from a past ignorance, an eating of the forbidden fruit as an entry into Eden rather than as an expulsion from it.

But, given the violence, disrespect, emotional chaos, lack of community, sexual irresponsibility, despondency, cynicism, and lack of delight in our world today, our generation might want to rethink its negative assessment of chastity. It might also (should it ever summon the courage) sort out what in the area of sexuality is victory and what is defeat.

From this we see that chastity is not to be identified with celibacy. One can be celibate, and not chaste; just as someone can be having sex and be chaste. My parents were two of the most chaste people I have ever known, and they enjoyed a healthy sex life. Chastity has to do with the way we relate to reality and life in general.

To be chaste means not opening our Christmas gifts before Christmas, not rushing our own or our children's growth, not experiencing things for which we aren't ready, not losing patience in life or in sex because there is tension, not violating someone else's beauty and sexual integrity, not applying a candle to a moth emerging from its cocoon because we're in a hurry, and not sleeping with the bride before the wedding. To be chaste is to let gift be gift. Every form of irreverence, disrespect, and impatience is the antithesis of chastity.

Chastity as a practical virtue is predicated on two things: patience and the capacity to carry tension. Indeed, patience is virtually synonymous with chastity. To fully respect others and the proper order of things means to be patient. Something can be wrong for no other reason than because it is premature. To do anything prematurely, whether that be growing up, or having sex, does what applying extra heat does to the process of metamorphosis. It makes for damaged wings.

To wait in tension, in incompleteness, in longing, in frustration, in inconsummation, and in patience in the face of the slowness of things is to practice chastity. When Jesus sweated blood in the Garden of Gethsemane, he was practicing chastity. Chastity's challenge reads this way: never short-circuit the process of metamorphosis. Whether you are dealing with sex or with life in general, wait for the wedding night for consummation.

Carlo Carretto, one of the great spiritual writers of recent times, spent many years alone as a hermit in the Sahara Desert. During these long, quiet years, he tried to hear what God was saying, and after all those years he was asked by a journalist, "What is the single most important thing you would want to say to the world after all that time in solitude, trying to hear God's voice? What is God saying to us?" Carretto replied, "God is saying this: *'Be patient! Learn to wait, to wait for everything: each other, love, happiness, God.'*"

CHAPTER 2

Chastity as Purity of Heart

To live a chaste life is not easy for anyone. Even when our outward actions are in line, it is still hard to live with a chaste heart, a chaste attitude, and chaste fantasies. Purity of heart and intention is very difficult.

Why? Chastity is difficult because we are so incurably sexual in every pore of our being. And that is not a bad thing. It's God's gift. Far from being something dirty and antithetical to our spiritual lives, sexuality is God's great gift, God's holy fire, inside us. And so, the longing for consummation is a conscious or inchoate coloring underlying most every action in our lives.

And so, it is hard to desire chastity because to desire it, seemingly, is to desire that sexual yearning and sexual energy should lessen within us or disappear altogether. And who wants to live an asexual and neutered life? No healthy person wants this. Thus, if you are healthy, it is hard to put your heart into truly longing for chastity because, deep down, nobody wants to be asexual.

But the problem is not with chastity but with our understanding of it. To be chaste does not mean that we become asexual (though spirituality has forever struggled not to make that equation). Chastity is not about denying our sexuality but about properly channeling it. To be chaste is to be pure of heart. That's the biblical notion of chastity. Jesus does not ask us to pray for chastity, he asks us to pray for "purity of heart": *Blessed are the pure in heart, for they shall see God* (NRSVCE). They will channel their sexuality properly.

What is purity of heart? To be pure of heart is to relate to others and the world in a way that respects and honors the full dignity, value, and destiny of every person and every thing. To be pure of heart is to see others as God sees them. Purity of heart would have us loving others with their good (and not our own) in mind. Karl Rahner suggests that we are pure of heart when we see others against an infinite horizon, namely, inside of a vision that sees the other's dignity, individuality, life, dreams, and sexuality within the biggest ambiance of all: God's eternal plan. Purity of heart is purity of intention and full respect in love.

When we understand chastity in this way, we can more easily pray for it. In this understanding we are not praying to have our sexual energies deadened, we are praying instead to remain fully red-blooded but with our sexual energies, intentions, and daydreams properly channeled. We are praying too for the kind of maturity, human and sexual, that fully respects others. In essence, we are praying for a deeper respect, a deeper maturity, and a more life-giving love.

And this is a much-needed prayer in our lives because sexuality is so powerful that even inside of a marriage relationship, sexuality can still have an intentionality that is not wide enough. Charles Taylor, in his book *A Secular Age*, argues that sex too easily loses the big picture and becomes too narrow in its focus, a point that is often missed in our understanding of it. He writes:

> I am not trying to be condescending about our ancestors, because I think that there is a real tension involved in trying to combine in one life sexual fulfillment and piety. This is only one of the points at which a more general tension, between human flourishing in general and dedication to God, makes itself felt. That this tension should be particularly evident in the sexual domain is readily understandable. Intense and profound sexual fulfillment focuses us powerfully on the exchange within the couple; it strongly attaches us possessively to what is privately shared. It is not for nothing that the early monks and hermits saw sexual renunciation as opening the way to the wider love of God. . . . That there is a tension between fulfillment and piety should not surprise us in a world distorted by sin, that is separated from God. But we have to avoid turning this into a constitutive incompatibility.

Unfortunately, that is forever what both the secular world and Christian spirituality struggle not to do.

Given the power of sexuality inside us, and given the power of our human drives and yearnings in general, it is not easy to live a chaste life. It is even more difficult, and rare, to have a chaste spirit, a chaste heart, chaste daydreams, and chaste intentions. Our hearts want what they want and pressure us to ignore the consequences. We can easily feel a certain repugnance to desiring to be chaste. But that is largely because we do not understand chastity: It is not a deadening of the heart, a stripping away of our sexuality, but a deeper maturity that lets our sexual energies flow out in a more life-giving way.

CHAPTER 3

Chastity, Love, and Sex

Woe to chastity that is not practiced out of love, but woe to love that excludes chastity.

These are the words of Benoit Standaert, a Benedictine monk, and I believe they can be profitably read in our culture today where, to the detriment of everyone, the sexually active and vowed celibates alike, sexuality and chastity are generally seen as opposed to each other, as enemies.

Unfortunately, this opposition is not very well understood today, either in our culture or in our churches. In our current culture, chastity is mostly seen as a naïveté, a lack of critical sophistication, a quality you honor and protect only in children. Indeed, within the popular culture today, chastity is often disdained and seen as a fear-based moral rigidity. Ironically, many of us in our churches who are trying to defend chastity are no healthier. We never link the chastity we defend to a spirituality that's wholesome enough to be able to celebrate sexuality as a beautiful gift from God that's intended to be linked to exuberance, spirituality, and delight.

Sexuality and chastity aren't enemies as our culture and churches make them out to be. They are different sides of the same coin. They need each other. Sexuality without chastity is invariably soulless and not respectful. Conversely, chastity that sees itself as somehow above or divorced from sex will invariably end up in sterility, judgment, and anger. Woe to either if it doesn't take the other seriously.

Unfortunately, with few exceptions, our churches have never understood sexuality well, just as our culture, with even fewer exceptions, has never grasped chastity well. One searches, mostly in vain, for a Christian spirituality of sexuality that's truly wholesome and which properly honors the wonderful gift God gave us in our sexuality. Likewise, one searches, also entirely in vain, for a secular voice that grasps the importance of chastity.

Sexuality, as we know, is more than sex. When God created the first human beings, God looked at them and said: "It's not good for a person to be alone!" That wasn't just true for Adam and Eve, it's true for every human being, every living thing, and every molecule and atom in the universe. It's not good to be alone, and sexuality is the fire within us that at every level of our being, conscious and unconscious, body and soul, drives us outward beyond our aloneness, toward family, community, friendship, companionship, procreation, co-creation, celebration, delight, and consummation. Sexuality is linked to our very instinct to continue breathing and cannot be separated from the sacredness we feel as creatures made in the image and likeness of God. As an energy, sexuality is sacred, never to be denigrated in the name of something higher nor reduced to the casual.

Chastity, as was emphasized earlier, is proper respect and proper patience, not just for how we stand before sex, but for how we stand before all of life. As well, as affirmed earlier, chastity is not the same thing as celibacy, much less frigidity. One can be celibate, but not chaste; just as one can be sexually active, and chaste. Properly understood, chastity is not anti-sexual; it strives to protect sexuality from its own excessive power by surrounding it with the needed filters—patience and respect, thus allowing the other person to be fully herself or himself, allowing us to be fully ourselves, and allowing sex to be what it was intended to be, a sacred, life-giving gift.

Sexuality and chastity need each other. Sexuality brings the energy, the longing, the fire, and the urgency that keep us aware, consciously and unconsciously, that it's not good to be alone. If we shut that off, we become sterile and angry. Chastity, on the other hand, tells us that, in that process of seeking union with all that's beyond us, we must have enough patience and respect to let the other fully be other and ourselves be fully ourselves.

CHAPTER 4

Chastity and Innocence

I n the rite for Christian baptism there's a little ritual that is at once both touching and unrealistic. At one point in the baptismal rite, the child is clothed in a white garment symbolizing innocence and purity. The priest or minister officiating says these words: "Receive this baptismal garment and bring it unstained to the judgment seat of our Lord Jesus Christ."

As touching as it is to say those words to an innocent baby, one cannot help but think that unless this child dies in childhood, this is an impossible task. Our baptismal robes inevitably take on some stains. Adult life sees to that. No one goes through life without losing the innocence of a baby.

But that being admitted, innocence remains an ideal to be fostered and continually recovered. And that needs some defense today because innocence and its attendants—purity and chastity—have fallen on hard times in a world that tends to value sophistication above all else and that generally sees innocence as naïveté and prudery.

There's a long history to this. For centuries, the churches held up innocence, purity, and chastity as salient virtues within Christian discipleship and within life in general. However, from the seventeenth century onward, right down to our own time, major thinkers have tried to turn this on its head, suggesting that these (so-called) virtues are in fact the antithesis of virtue, fraudulent ideals, fantasies of the timid, and symptoms of an unconscious hostility toward life.

Friedrich Nietzsche, for example, once wrote: "The church combats the passions with excision, in every sense of the word: its practice, its cure, is castration." Sigmund Freud suggested that in the ideals of innocence, purity, and chastity, there is more than a trace of narcissism, frigid arrogance, and a fantasy of invulnerability. According to these (*Enlightenment*) thinkers, in idealizing innocence, purity, and chastity, humankind has agreed to make itself unhappy in that the medicine we take to purify our souls lets in the moral toxins of self-righteousness, arrogance, and insensitivity, a mischief that makes lust look benign.

Our culture essentially buys into this. Where to go with all of this? Well, one isn't quite sure where to look.

Conservatives, in their very makeup, tend to fear the breaking of taboos, not least those surrounding innocence, purity, and chastity. This has a healthy intent. This is J. D. Salinger (*The Catcher in the Rye*) looking at innocent young children playing and wishing they would never grow up but could always remain this innocent and joyful. Conservatives tend to fear any kind of sophistication that destroys innocence. That's well intended but unrealistic. We need to grow up, and with that comes complexity, sophistication, mess, and stains on the purity of our baptismal robes. God did not intend for us to be children forever playing in innocence in a rye field.

Liberals have a different genetic make-up, but struggle equally (just differently) with innocence, purity, and chastity. They are less fearful about breaking taboos. For them, boundaries are meant to be stretched and most times broken, and innocence is a phase you pass through and outgrow (like belief in Santa and the Easter Bunny). Indeed, for liberals, real self-actualization begins with owning your complexity, recognizing its goodness, and accepting that complexity and lost innocence are in fact what open us up for deeper meaning.

Experience brings knowledge. When Adam and Eve ate the forbidden fruit, their eyes were opened, not closed. To the liberal eye, naïveté is not a virtue, sophistication is. Innocence is judged as unrealistic, purity as sexual timidity, and chastity as religious fundamentalism.

Both these views, conservative and liberal, wave some healthy warning flags. The conservative flag of caution can help save us from many self-destructive behaviors, while the liberal flag inviting us to more fearlessness can help save us from much unhealthy timidity and naïveté. However, each needs to learn from the other. Conservatives need to learn that God did not intend for us to make an idol out of the innocence and the naïveté of a child. We are meant to learn, to grow, and to become sophisticated beyond first naïveté. But liberals need to learn that sophistication, like innocence, is not an end in itself, but a phase through which one grows.

The renowned contemporary philosopher Paul Ricoeur hints at something beyond both. He asserts that growth to final maturity goes through stages. We are meant to move from the naïveté of a child, through the messy and often cynical sophistication of adulthood, toward a "second naïveté," a post-sophistication, a second innocence, a childlikeness that is not childish, a simplicity that is not simplistic.

In this second naïveté, our baptismal robes will emerge again unstained—washed clean in the blood of a new innocence.

CHAPTER 5

Sublimation and the Sublime

In the early 1990s, Robert Waller published a book that became a runaway bestseller and an immensely popular movie. *The Bridges of Madison County* stirred the romantic imagination in a way that few other stories have in recent times, especially as it was played out in its film version. The story runs this way.

A photographer for *National Geographic* magazine is sent out to photograph a series of old bridges in Madison County. Lost, he stops at a farmhouse to ask for directions. As chance would have it, the man of the house is absent. His wife is home alone, and she and the photographer instantly sense a deep connection and fall deeply in love. Karma, soulmates, mysticism, whatever, they experience a rare and powerful affinity. Within hours they are in bed with each other, triggering a love affair that leaves them both emotionally scarred for the rest of their lives.

What the viewer of the movie or reader of this book is asked to believe is that something truly sublime has taken place, a masterpiece of love has been painted, and a noble thing worth more than life itself has just occurred. But can this be so? Can anyone paint a masterpiece in a couple of hours? Can a doctoral thesis be completed in two hours? Can sex with someone you have known for just two hours be sublime?

As a contrasting narrative to this, I suggest another film which, ironically, was playing in theatres at nearly the same time. It's a version of Jane Austin's *Sense and Sensibility*, and it tells the story of a young woman who has to carry a very painful tension (one that includes the same obsessive, mystical feelings found in *Bridges of Madison County*) for a long time. But unlike the characters in *Bridges of Madison County*, she doesn't move quickly to resolve it. She is not in bed with her lover within a couple of hours. She carries the tension for a long time, years, and then finally when it is resolved, there is true sublimity. Why? Because something can be sublime only if first there has been some sublimation (and for more than two hours!).

What is the connection? How does carrying tension help lead to the sublime? A metaphor might be helpful here. In carrying tension, metaphorically we come to kindling temperature and are made ready for love. Pierre Teilhard de Chardin, a renowned scientist and theologian, noted that sometimes when you put two chemicals into a test tube they do not automatically unite. They only merge at a higher temperature. They must first be heated to bring about unity. There's an anthropology and psychology of love in that image. In order to experience the sublime, there must first be some sublimation; we must first be brought to a higher psychic temperature. What brings us there? Sizzling in tension, not resolving things prematurely, not sleeping with the bride before the wedding, not trying to have the complete symphony within two hours.

The sublime has to be waited for. To give birth to what's divine requires the slow patience of gestation.

CHAPTER 6

The Goddess of Chastity

ncient Greece expressed much of its psychological and spiritual wisdom in their myths. They didn't intend these to be taken literally or as historical, but as metaphor and as an archetypal illustration of why life is as it is and how people engage life both generatively and destructively.

And many of these myths are centered on gods and goddesses. They had gods and goddesses to mirror virtually every aspect of life, every aspect of human behavior, and every innate human propensity. Moreover, many of these gods and goddesses were far from moral in their behavior, especially in their sexual lives. They had messy affairs with each other and with human beings. However, despite the messiness and amorality of their sexual behavior, one of the positive features in these myths was that, for Ancient Greece, sex was always, somehow, connected to the divine. Even temple prostitution was somehow related to accessing the fertility that emanated from the divine realm.

Within this pantheon of gods and goddesses there was a particular goddess named Artemis. Unlike most of their other goddesses, who were sexually promiscuous, she was chaste and celibate. Her sexual abstinence represented the place and the value of chastity and celibacy. She was pictured as a tall, graceful figure, attractive sexually, but with a beauty that, while sexual, was different from the seductive sexuality of goddesses like Aphrodite and Hera. In the figure of Artemis, sex is pictured as an attractive blend of solitude and integrity. She is frequently pictured surrounded by members of her own sex or by members of the opposite sex who appear as friends and intimates, but never as lovers.

What's implied here is that sexual desire can remain healthy and generative even while abstaining from sex. Artemis represents a chaste way of being sexual. She tells us that, in the midst of a sexually soaked world, one can be generative and happy inside of chastity and even inside celibacy. Perhaps even more importantly, Artemis shows us that chastity need not render one antisexual and sterile. Rather she shows that sexuality is wider than sex and that sex itself will be richer and more meaningful if it is also connected to chastity. Artemis declares that claiming your solitude and experiencing friendship and other forms of intimacy are not a substitute for sex but one of the rich modalities of sex itself.

Thomas Moore, in describing Artemis, writes: "Although she is the most virginal of the goddesses, Artemis is not asexual. She embodies a special kind of sexuality where the accent is on individuality, integrity, and solitude." As such, she is a model not just for celibates but also for people who are sexually active. For a sexually active person, Artemis is the cautionary flag that says: I want to be taken seriously, with my integrity and independence assured.

As well, Moore suggests that, irrespective of whether we are celibate or sexually active, we all "have periods in life or just moments in a day when we need to be alone, disconnected from love and sex, devoted to an interest of our own, withdrawn and remote. Artemis tells us that this preference may not be an antisocial rejection of people but simply a deep, positive, even sexual focusing of oneself and one's world."

What's taught by this mythical goddess is a much-needed lesson for our world today. Our age has turned sex into a soteriology, namely, for us, sex isn't perceived as a means towards heaven, it is identified with heaven itself. It's what we're supposed to be living for. One of the consequences of this is that we can no longer blend our adult awareness with chastity, nor with the genuine complexity and richness of sex. Rather, for many of us, chastity and celibacy are seen as a fearful self-protection, which leave one dry, sterile, moralistic, anti-erotic, sexually uptight, and on the periphery of life's joys. Tied to this too is the notion that all those rich realities so positively highlighted by Artemis (as well as by the classical Christian notion of chastity), namely, friendship, nonsexual forms of intimacy, nonsexual pleasures, and the need for integrity and fidelity within sex, are seen as a substitute for sex, and a second-best one at that, rather than as a rich modality of sex itself.

We are psychologically and spiritually impoverished by that notion, and it puts undue pressure on our sexual lives. When sex is asked to carry the primary load in terms of human generativity and happiness, it cannot help but come up short. And we are seeing that in our world today.

Of course, as Christians, we have our own goddesses of chastity: Mary, the mother of Jesus, and many women saints. Why not draw our spirituality of chastity from these women, rather than looking towards some pagan, mythical goddess? Well, for the most part, we do look to Christian models here. Moreover, I suspect that both the Virgin Mary and all our revered virgin saints would, were she actually a real person, very much befriend Artemis.

CHAPTER 7

Chastity as Blessing Others

Although not too many people might recognize this, the *#MeToo* movement is, in essence, a strong advocate for chastity. If chastity can be defined as standing before another with reverence, respect, and patience, then most everything about the *#MeToo* movement speaks explicitly of the nonnegotiable importance of chastity, and implicitly for what our sexuality is ultimately meant to do, namely, to bless others rather than to exploit them.

What the *#MeToo* movement has helped expose is how sex is often used as power, power to force sexual consent, power to either allow or block someone from advancement in her life and career, and power to make someone's workplace a place of comfort and safety or a place of discomfort and fear. This has been going on since the beginning of time and remains the sexual tool today of many people in positions of power and prestige: Hollywood directors, television personalities, university professors, famous athletes, employers, spiritual leaders, and persons of every kind who wield power and prestige.

Too often, persons with power and prestige let themselves (however unconsciously) be taken over by the ancient and medieval notion of the king, where the belief was that all the women in the land belonged to the king and he had sexual privilege by divine right. The *#MeToo* movement is saying that this time in history is over and something else is being asked from persons in power, authority, and prestige. What's being asked? Given the existence of power and given the dynamics of sex, what is being called for? What is to be the proper interplay between power and sex?

In a word, *blessing*. What God and nature ask of power is that it bless rather than exploit, use privilege to enhance rather than harass, and create a space/place of security rather than a place of fear.

Imagine, for example, if in every one of those high-profile instances where a Hollywood producer, a major television personality, or a star athlete was indicted for harassing, exploiting, and assaulting women, those men, wielding power and prestige, had used that power instead to help those women gain more access to security and success rather than (pardon the terminology) "hitting on them." Imagine if they had used their power to bless those women, to simply admire their beauty and energy, make them feel safe, and help them in their careers. How different things would be today both for those women and for those men. Both would be happier, healthier, and have a deeper appreciation of sex. Why? What's the connection between blessing and sex?

To bless a person is, first of all, to give that person the gaze of nonexploitive admiration, to admire him or her without an angle of self-interest. Next, to bless someone is to use your own power and prestige to help make that other person's life more safe and secure and help that person flourish in his or her dreams and endeavors. To bless another person is to say to him or her: *I delight in your beauty and your energy—and what can I do for you that helps you and isn't in my self-interest?* To bless another in this way is the highest expression of sexuality and of chastity. How so?

Sexuality is more than sex and chastity is more than sexual abstinence. Sexuality is the drive in us for community, friendship, wholeness, family, creativity, play, transpersonal meaning, altruism, enjoyment, delight, sexual fulfilment, immortality, and everything that takes us beyond our aloneness. But this has developmental stages. Its earlier stages focus on having sex, on intimacy, and on generativity, on giving birth and nurturing. Its later stages focus on blessing, on admiration, and on giving away so that others might have more.

Dare I say this? The most mature expression of sexuality on this planet is not a couple making perfect love, wonderful and sacred though that is. Rather, it is a grandparent looking at a grandchild with a love that is purer and more selfless than any love he or she has ever experienced, a love without any self-interest, which is only admiration, selflessness, and delight. In that moment, this person is mirroring God looking at the initial creation and exclaiming: It is good;

it is very good! What follows then is that this person, like God, will try to open paths, even at the cost of death, so that another's life may flourish.

Blessing others is not just the ultimate expression of sexuality, it is also the ultimate path to properly order and channel our sexual energies. When we bless another person we, in a manner of speaking, *cauterize* our earthier natural instincts vis-à-vis sex and our propensity for ego gratification.

The renowned mystic John of the Cross articulates this well in his spirituality of healing. For him, you overcome the sometimes-overpowering pressures of your natural instincts not by denying them or repressing them, but by cauterizing them (his terminology), that is, by stretching them to their highest intentionality. The greater good is what puts everything else in perspective, and achieving it is what creates genuine delight and joy in our lives.

As we saw, God and nature intended sex for many purposes—intimacy, delight, generativity, community, and pleasure—and thus it has many expressions. Perhaps its ultimate expression is that of admiration, of someone looking at another person or at the world with the sheer gaze of admiration, with everything inside that person somehow saying: *Wow! I delight in you! Your energy touches my heart! What can I do to help you?* The higher integrates and cauterizes the lower. There are no temptations to violate the beauty and dignity of the other when we can give her or him the sheer gaze of admiration.

Admiration is the endgame of chastity. Would that those in power indicted by the *#MeToo* movement had admired rather than exploited.

PART TWO

Chastity, Sex, and the Soul

Monogamous sex is a small price for so great a gift as the wonder and ecstasy of meeting another in so deep a fashion.

To surround sex with chastity is like surrounding anything of importance with its proper reverence. Generally, we understand this more with our hearts than with our heads. For instance, the classical symbols that surround a wedding ceremony—a church, sacred vows, rings, a white dress, maids and gentlemen of honor, a minister of church or state presiding, a banquet complete with toasts—heighten the sublimity of the event and make it special. We feel this more than think it. Weddings that cheat on the symbols don't evoke the same measure of honest tears. Proper symbols raise the mundane and make it sublime.

Most of our major rituals around the ceremony of marriage are in fact symbols that, in that context, are predicated on chastity. They celebrate initial sexual union *and highlight its importance both for the couple marrying and for society at large. The bride's white dress, for example, is a symbol of chastity and its task (which it does well) is to heighten, not lessen, the passion for sex. A bride's dress speaks of the sublime, to assure that this day is truly special. One can get married in old blue jeans and a torn t-shirt and have the ceremony be over in two minutes, but such a ceremony will be a fault in chastity because it will do little to heighten our passion, highlight the sublimity of sex, or mark this exchange of vows as a pivotal moment within one's life.*

CHAPTER 8

A Plea for the Soul

It's hard to find your soulmate in someone who doesn't believe you have a soul.

Recently on a radio program, a young woman shared the story of her breakup with her boyfriend, a young man for whom she had deep feelings. The problem was that she, a person with a deep Mormon faith, struggled with the radical materialism of her boyfriend. For him, there were no souls; the physical world was real and nothing else. She kept asking him if he believed he had a soul. He couldn't make himself believe that. Eventually, not without a lot of heartache, they broke up. Why? *In her words: It's hard to find your soulmate in someone who doesn't believe you have a soul.*

Her frustration is becoming more universal. More and more our world is ignoring and denying the existence of soul and is becoming soulless. It wasn't always like this. Up until modern times, often it was the physical and the body that weren't properly honored. But things have changed, radically.

It began with Darwin, who rooted our origins more in the history of our bodies than in the origins of our souls.

It took more shape in the mechanistic philosophies of the last century, which understood both our universe and ourselves as physical machines. It became more firm as modern medicine and experimental psychology began more and more to explain the brain primarily in terms of carbon complexification and biochemical interactions. It seeped into our higher educational systems as we produced more and more technical schools rather than universities in the deeper sense. And it culminated in popular culture, where love and sex are spoken of more in terms of chemistry than in terms of soul. It is not surprising that for most pop singers today the mantra is: *I want your body! I want your body!* We're a long way from Shakespeare's marriage of true minds and Yeats's love of the pilgrim soul in you.

Religion, of course, has always lodged its protests against this, but often its understanding of the soul was itself too narrow to have much power to lure a materialistic culture back into wanting to rediscover and listen to the soul. Ironically, it took a nonreligious figure, Carl Jung, to speak of soul again in a way that is intellectually intriguing. And it was in the sick, the insane, the suicidal, and others whose lives were broken that Jung began to hear the cry of the soul (whose demands are sometimes very different from those of the body and whose needs are for much more than simple comfort and the prolonging of life).

Much of Jung's teaching and that of his followers can be seen as a protest for the soul. We see this, for example, in the writing of James Hillman. It's ironic that as an agnostic he was able to speak about the soul in ways that we, who are religious, might envy and emulate. Like Jung, he also drew many of his insights from listening to the soul cry out its meaning and pain through the voices of the sick, the insane, the broken, and the suicidal. Religion, medicine, and psychology, he believes, are not hearing the soul's cry. They're forever trying to fix the soul, cure the soul, or save the soul, rather than listening to the soul, which wants and needs neither to be fixed nor saved. It's already eternal. The soul needs to be heard, and heard in all its godly goodness and earthy complexity. And sometimes what it tells us goes against all common sense, medical practice, and the oversimplistic spiritualities we often present as religion.

To be more in touch with our souls we might examine an older language, the language that religion, poets, mythologists, and lovers used before today's dominant materialism turned our language about the soul into the language of chemistry and mechanism. We cannot understand the soul through any scientific description but only by looking at its behavior, its insatiability, its dissatisfactions, and its protests. A soul isn't explained, it's experienced, and soul experience always comes soaked in depth, in longing, in eros, in limit, in the feeling of being a pilgrim in need of a soulmate.

Happily, even today, we still do spontaneously connect the soul to things beyond chemistry and mechanism. As Hillman points out, we associate the word "soul" with mind, spirit, heart, life, warmth, humanness, personality, individuality, intentionality, essence, innermost, purpose, emotion, quality, virtue, morality, sin, wisdom, death, God. As well, we speak of a soul as "troubled," "old," "disembodied," "immortal," "lost," "innocent," "inspired." Eyes are said to be "soulful," for the eyes are "the mirror of the soul"; and one can be "soulless" by showing no mercy.

Soullessness: We understand the makeup of something best when we see it broken. So perhaps today we can best understand our soullessness in the growing acceptance of pornography and hook-up sex, where the soul is intentionally and necessarily excluded from what is meant to be the epitome of all soulful experience.

Amia Srinivasan, in a book entitled *The Right to Sex*, shares the story of a colleague, a university lecturer, who sees no big ethical or psychological issue with sleeping with one of his students. His rationalization: what's the difference between this and a professor playing a game of tennis with his student? Sex needn't be special unless you want it to be special. What makes sex different from a game of tennis?

Only someone dangerously naïve does not see a huge *soulful* difference here. A game of tennis does not touch the soul with any depth. Sex does, and not just because some churches say so. We see this when it is violated. Recall how Freud once said that we understand things most clearly when we see them broken. Nowhere is this clearer than in how sexual violence and exploitive sex affect a person. When sex is wrong, there is violation of soul that dwarfs anything that ever results from a tennis game.

Sex is not soulful because some churches say so. It's soulful because it's connected to the soul in ways that tennis isn't. Ironically, just as the culture is trivializing society's traditional view on sex as innately soulful, persons working with those suffering sexual trauma are seeing ever more clearly how exploitive sex is on a radically different plane, in terms of soul, than playing tennis with someone.

Chastity is a plea for the soul.

CHAPTER 9

Our Dark Memory of Our Soul

Inside each of us, beyond what we can express in words, picture clearly, or even feel distinctly, we have a dark memory of having once been touched and caressed by hands far gentler than our own. That caress has left a permanent mark, the imprint of a love so tender and good that its memory becomes a prism through which we see everything else. This imprint lies beyond conscious memory but forms the center of the heart and soul.

This is not an easy concept to explain. Bernard Lonergan, one of the great intellectuals of the past century, tried to explain it philosophically. He said that we bear inside our souls "the brand of the first principles." That's accurate, but perhaps too abstract to grasp. Maybe the old myths and legends capture it best when they say that, before birth, each soul is kissed by God and then goes through life always in some dark way remembering that kiss and measuring everything it experiences in relation to that original sweetness. To be in touch with your heart is to be in touch with this primordial kiss, with both its preciousness and its meaning.

What exactly is being said here?

Within each of us, at that place where all that is most precious within us resides, there is an inchoate sense of having once been touched, caressed, loved, and valued in a way that is beyond anything we have ever consciously experienced. In fact, all the goodness, love, value, and tenderness we experience in life fall short precisely because we already know something deeper. When we feel frustrated, angry, betrayed, violated, or enraged, it is in fact because our outside experience is so different from what we already hold dear inside.

We all have this place, a place in the heart, where we hold all that is most precious and sacred to us. From that place our own kisses issue forth, as do our tears. It is the place that we most guard from others, but the place where we would most want others to come into, the place where we are the most deeply alone and the place of intimacy, the place of innocence and the place where we are violated, the place of our compassion and the place of our rage. In that place we are holy. There we are temples of God, sacred churches of truth and love. It is there that we bear God's image.

But this must be understood: The image of God inside us is not some beautiful icon stamped inside the soul. No. The image and likeness of God inside us is energy, fire, memory—especially the memory of a touch so tender and loving that its goodness and truth become the prism through which we see everything. Thus we recognize goodness and truth outside us precisely because they resonate with something that is already inside us. Things touch our hearts when they touch us here and it is because we have already been touched and caressed that we seek passionately for a soulmate, for someone to join us in this tender space.

And we measure everything in life by how it touches this place: Why do certain experiences touch us so deeply? Do not our hearts burn within us in the presence of any truth, love, goodness, or tenderness that is genuine and deep? Is not all deep knowledge simply a waking up to something we already know? Is not all love simply a question of being respected for something we already are? Are not the touch and tenderness that bring ecstasy nothing other than the stirring of deep memory? Are not the ideals that inspire hope only the reminder of words somebody has already spoken to us? Does not our desire for innocence (and innocent means "not wounded") mirror some primal unwounded place deep within us? And when we feel violated, is it not because someone has irreverently entered the sacred inside us?

When we are in touch with this memory and respect its sensitivities, we are feeling our souls. At those times, faith, hope, and love will spring up in us, and both joy and tears will flow through us freely. We will be constantly stabbed by the innocence and beauty of children, and pain and gratitude will, alternately, bring us to our knees. That is what it means to be recollected, centered. To be truly ourselves is to remember, to inchoately touch and feel the memory of God in us. That memory is what both fires our energy and provides us with a prism through which to see and understand.

Today, too often, a wounded, calloused, cynical, oversophisticated, and overly adult world invites us to forget, to move beyond this childishness (which is really childlikeness). It invites us to forget God's kiss of the soul. But, unless we lie to ourselves and harden ourselves against ourselves, the most dangerous of all activities, we will always remember, dimly, darkly, the caress of God.

CHAPTER 10

Sex and the Soul

During the Nazi occupation of France during World War II, a group of Jesuit theologians who were resisting the occupation published an underground newspaper, *Cahiers du Témoignage Chrétien*, which had a famous opening line in its first issue: *"France, take care not to lose your soul."* That brought to mind a comment I once heard from Peter Hans Kolvenbach, then the Superior General of the Jesuits. Speaking of globalization, he commented that one of the things he feared about globalization was the *globalization of triviality*. Fair warning!

Today we are witnessing a trivialization of soul within the culture. Few things are sublime anymore, meaning few things are soulful anymore. Things that used to have deep meaning are now related to more casually. Take sex, for instance. More and more (with a few churches being the sole holdouts) the culture believes that sex need not be soulful, unless you want it to be and personally invest it with such meaning.

Sex is soulful, and we see this clearly when we see how sexual violence and exploitative sex affect a person. Ironically, just as the culture is trivializing society's traditional view on sex as innately soulful, persons working with those suffering sexual trauma are seeing ever more clearly how exploitive sex is on a radically different plane in terms of its effects on soul.

However, it's not just that we are trivializing the soulful; we are also struggling to hear our souls. It's noteworthy that today this warning is coming not as much from the churches as from a wide range of voices from agnostic philosophers to Jungian analysts. For example, the *leitmotif* in the writings of the agnostic philosopher of soul James Hillman is that the task of life is to live soulfully, and we can do that only by truly listening to our souls. And, he submits, there's a lot at stake here. In a book entitled *Suicide and the Soul*, he suggests that what sometimes happens in a suicide is that the soul, unable to make its cries heard, eventually kills the body.

Depth psychology offers similar insights and suggests that the presence in our lives of certain symptoms like depression, excess anxiety, guilt disorders, and the need to self-medicate are often the soul's cries to be heard. James Hollis suggests that sometimes when we have bad dreams it's because our soul is angry with us, and that in the face of these symptoms (depression, anxiety, guilt, bad dreams) we need to ask ourselves: *"What does my soul want from me?"*

Indeed, what do our souls want from us? They want many things, though in essence, they want three things: *to be protected*, *to be honored*, and *to be listened to*.

First, our souls need to be protected from violation and trivialization. What lies deepest inside us, at the center of our souls, is something Thomas Merton once described as *le point vierge* (the "virgin point"). All that is most sacred, tender, true, and vulnerable in us is housed there, and while our souls send us constant cries wanting protection, they cannot protect themselves. They need us to protect their *point vierge*.

Second, our souls need to be honored, their sacredness fully respected, and their depth properly recognized. Our soul is the "burning bush" before which we need to stand with our shoes off, reverent. To lose that reverence is to trivialize our own depth.

Finally, our souls need to be listened to. Their cries, their beckonings, their resistances, and the dreams they give us while we sleep need to be heard. Moreover, they need to be heard not only when they are buoyant, but also when they are heavy, sad, and angry. As well, we need to hear both their plea for protection and their challenge to us to take risks.

Soul is a precious thing worth protecting. It's the deepest voice inside us, speaking for what's most important and most soulful in our lives, and so we need ever to heed the warning: *take care not to lose your soul.*

Chastity protects the soul.

CHAPTER 11

Chastity as Soulful and Taking Us Home

During the years that I served as a Religious Superior for a province of Oblate Priests and Brothers in Western Canada, I tried to keep my foot in the academic world by doing some adjunct teaching at the University of Saskatchewan. It was always a once-a-week, night course, advertised as a primer on Christian theology, and it drew a variety of students.

One of the assigned readings for that course was Christopher de Vinck's book *Only the Heart Knows How to Find Them: Precious Memories for a Faithless Time*. The book is a series of autobiographical essays, most of which focus on his home life and his relationship with his wife and children. The essays describing his relationship to his wife don't overplay the romantic, but they are wonderfully heartwarming and set sex within a context of marriage, safety, and fidelity.

At the end of the semester a young woman, 30 years old, commented as she handed in her term paper, a reflection on de Vinck's book: "This is the best book I've ever read. I didn't have a lot of moral guidance growing up and so I wasn't always careful with my heart and was pretty free and existential about sex. I've basically slept my way through two Canadian provinces; but now I know that what I really want is what this man has. I need sex to take me home, not to be a place that I go home from. I'm looking for the marriage bed!" Her eyes teared as she shared this.

I'm looking for the marriage bed! That's a great image for what the heart calls home.

At the end of the day, what is home? Is it an ethnic identity, a gender, a citizenship, a house somewhere, the place where we were born, or is it a place in the heart?

It's a place in the heart, and the image of the marriage bed situates it well. Home is where you are comfortable, physically, psychologically, and morally. Home is where you feel safe. Home is where your heart doesn't feel out of place, compromised, violated, denigrated, trivialized, or pushed aside (even if it is sometimes taken for granted). Home is a place you don't have to leave to be yourself. Home is where you can be fully yourself without the need to posture that you are anything other than who you are. Home is where you are at ease.

There are various lessons couched inside that concept of home, not least, as this young woman came to realize, some valuable insights vis-à-vis how we think about love and sex. Some of what's at stake here is captured in the popular notion of longing for a soulmate. The trouble though is that generally we tend to think of a soulmate in overly charged romantic terms. But, as de Vinck's books illustrate, finding a soulmate has more to do with finding the moral comfort and psychological safety of a monogamous marriage bed than it has to do with the stuff of romantic novels.

In terms of our sexuality, what lies deepest inside our erotic longings is the desire to find someone to take us home. Any sex from which you have to go home is still something that is not delivering what you most long for and is, at best, a temporary tonic that leaves you searching still for something further and more real.

The phrase *I'm looking for the marriage bed* also contains some insights vis-à-vis discerning among the various kinds of love, infatuation, and attractions we fall into. Most of us are by nature temperamentally promiscuous, meaning that we experience strong feelings of attraction, infatuation, and love for all kinds of others, irrespective of the fact that often what we are attracted to in another is not something we could ever be at home with. We can fall in love with a lot of different kinds of people, but what kind of love makes for a marriage and a home? Marriage and home are predicated on the kind of love that takes you home, on the kind of love that gives you the sense that with this person you can be at home and can build a home.

And, obviously, this concept doesn't just apply to a husband and wife in marriage. It's an image for what constitutes home—for everyone, married and celibate alike. *The marriage bed* is a metaphor for what puts one's psychological and moral center at ease.

T. S. Eliot once wrote: *Home is where we start from*. It's also where we want to end up. At birth our parents bring us home. That's where we start from and where we are at ease until puberty drives us out in search of another home. Lots of pitfalls potentially await us in that search, but if we listen to that deep counsel inside us, that irrepressible longing to get home again, then like the wise Magi who followed a special star to the manger, we too will find the marriage bed—or, at least, we won't be looking for it in all the wrong places.

Chastity is a GPS that can help guide us home.

CHAPTER 12

Santa, the Easter Bunny, Soul, and Chastity

Nearly forty years ago, the renowned educator Allan Bloom wrote a very provocative book entitled *The Closing of the American Mind*. As its title suggests, this isn't a book that flatters contemporary culture. Part of our mind is darkening, he suggests. Our sophistication is making us smarter but less wise. Something inside us is narrowing. What? What's narrowing inside us? How are our minds closing?

His basic idea can be captured in this autobiographical piece:

When he was a young undergraduate student in university, one of his professors walked into class on the first day and said to the students: "You come here from your parochial backgrounds, full of your childish beliefs; well, I am going to bathe you in the great truths and set you free!"

Bloom wasn't impressed. For him, this professor reminded him of a little boy who had solemnly informed him at age seven that there was no Santa Claus or Easter Bunny. However, Bloom adds, he wasn't bathing me in any great truths, just showing off, like the professor. But still the lesson wasn't lost on him. From this, Bloom resolved to teach in the exact opposite way. He would, on the first day of his classes, walk into the lecture room, look at his young students, and begin his class in words to this effect: "You come here with a lot of experience, already having tasted life, having been to a lot of places, and seen a lot of things, so I'm going to try to teach you how to believe in Santa Claus and the Easter Bunny again—then maybe you'll have a chance to be happy!"

This invitation, to learn how to believe in Santa and the Easter Bunny again, is not so much a challenge to come back to the innocence of a child (something we could never do, even if we tried) but to see the knowledge and maturity that we've gained from all our years of learning and experience not as an end but as a stage, a necessary one, on the journey to a still deeper place—wisdom, fuller maturity.

What that means is that it is not just important to learn and become sophisticated, it is equally important to eventually become post-sophisticated; it is not just important to grow in experience and shed naïveté, it is equally important to eventually find a certain "second naïveté"; and it is not just a sign of intelligence and maturity to stop believing in Santa and the Easter Bunny, it is a sign of even more intelligence and deeper maturity to start believing in them again.

An old philosophy professor of mine used to express this in this series of adages: *If you ask a naïve child if she believes in Santa and the Easter Bunny, she will say yes. If you ask a bright child the same question, she will say no. But if you ask an even brighter child that question, she will say yes, for another reason.*

But that's not an easy belief. To be an adult is precisely to be experienced, complex, wounded. To be an adult is to have lost one's innocence. None of us, unless we die very young, carries the dignity of our person and of our baptism unstained through life. We fall, we compromise, we sin, we get hurt, we hurt others, and mostly we grow ever more pathologically complex, with layer after layer of emotional and intellectual complexity separating us from the little girl and little boy who once believed in Santa and the Easter Bunny in innocence and joyful anticipation. And that can be painful.

Sometimes, if we're sensitive, the innocence of children can be like the stab of a knife to the soul, making us feel as if we've fallen from ourselves. But, in the end, that's an unhealthy over-idealization, the false nostalgia of J. D. Salinger's *Catcher in the Rye*. We're not meant to be children forever.

Sometimes, more positively, we get to experience our old innocence and youthful wonder vicariously in the eyes of our own children, in their joyful belief in Santa and the Easter Bunny, their anticipation and gleeful celebration of Christmas. Their belief can help us find a certain softness inside again—not at the same place where we once felt things when we were children and still believed in Santa (because that would only bring a painful stab of nostalgia), but at a new place, a place beyond where we define ourselves as grown up. That's where wisdom is born—and that's a place chastity can help us find.

CHAPTER 13

Sex, Our Private Lives, and the Evening News

*T*here is no such thing as a private act—whether sin or virtue. Everything we do, for good or for bad, has consequences for everyone else. Why do I say this?

The private is always social. When we watch the world news at night, what we see there, be it violence, greed, selfishness, grandiosity, lust, raw self-interest, flat-out human blindness or compassion, altruism, nobility of spirit, self-sacrifice, or brilliant ingenuity, reflects what's inside each of us. It is simply a mirror reflecting us back to ourselves. Nothing we see there should surprise us. Anyone who watches the world news and is scandalized and mystified by what is shown there is out of touch with what's inside him or her. What's outside simply reflects what's inside. The private is social. Humanity is one body, and everything we do impacts the whole body.

And for a Christian, this is further predicated on a doctrine that's central to our self-understanding, namely, the belief that we are the Body of Christ. As Christians, we believe that, with Jesus as our head, we form a community that is more than just a sociological reality. If Scripture is to be believed, the union we have with each other inside the Body of Christ is that of one living organism. We are that intimately in union with each other! And inside a living organism all parts affect all other parts. There are no private zones inside a live body, zones whose health or disease do not affect the whole body. If that is true, and it is, then indeed there is no such thing as a private act—sinful or virtuous.

In terms of an analogy, this might be explained this way: inside a living body there is an immune system. This is a complex network of cells, organs, proteins, enzymes, and tissues that are forever defending the body from harmful bacteria, viruses, parasites, and cancer cells. And each of these has an effect on the whole body. A cell, organ, protein, enzyme, or tissue is either helping bring health to the body or it is a cancerous cell working against the health of the body. No cell, organ, tissue, or enzyme can do anything that doesn't affect the whole body, for health or for disease.

However, this is more than an analogy. As members of the Body of Christ (and even just as members of the human race) we are cells, organs, proteins, enzymes, and tissues inside one immune system, and every act we do, no matter how seemingly private, affects the entire body, for good or for bad. No one has the luxury of ever doing a private act. If we are faithful in private, we help bring health to the whole body; if we are unfaithful in private, we bring harm to the whole body.

And this is particularly pertinent as it pertains to chastity. In a book entitled *The Road Is How: A Prairie*

Pilgrimage through Nature, Desire and Soul, Trevor Herriot suggests that how chaste we are in our private lives is more socially consequential that we normally imagine, that is, how we relate to each other and to ourselves sexually is more than a private affair. Here are his words:

> In a world bathed in industrial and impersonal sex, where real connection and tenderness are rare, will we sense also that something in us and in the earth is being harmed from the same absence of intimacy, care, and respect? Will we learn that any given expression of our erotic energies either connects us to or divides us from the world around us and our souls? We are discovering that we must steward the energies captured by nature in the hydrocarbons or in living plants and animals, and thereby improve the ways we receive the fruits of the earth, but we struggle to see the primary responsibility we bear for the small but cumulatively significant explosions of energy we access and transmit as we respond to our own longings to connect, merge, and be fruitful. Learning how to steward the way we bear fruit ourselves as spiritual/sexual beings with a full set of animal desires and angelic ambitions may be more important to the human journey than we fully understand.

How we treat others and ourselves sexually is inextricably connected to what is happening in our world. The evening news, at a point, reflects our sexual lives and the presence or absence of a healthy chastity within them.

CHAPTER 14

The Original Sin as a Failure in Chastity

The theologian James Mackey shared this story in class:

A man he knew was once part of a hunting expedition in Africa. One morning this man left the camp early, by himself, and hiked several miles into the jungle, where he surprised and eventually bagged two wild turkeys. Buckling his catch to his belt, he headed back to camp. At a point, however, he sensed he was being followed. With his senses sharpened by fright, he stopped, hands on his rifle, and looked around him. His fears were dispelled when he saw who was following him.

Following him at a distance was a naked, obviously starved adolescent boy. The boy's obvious objective was food, not threat. Seeing this, the man stopped, unbuckled his belt, and letting the turkeys fall to the ground, backed off and gestured to the boy that he could come and take the birds. The boy ran up to the two birds but, inexplicably, refused to pick them up. He was, seemingly, still asking for something else. Perplexed, the man tried both by words and by gestures to indicate to the boy that he could have the birds. Still the boy refused to pick them up. Finally, in desperation, unable to explain what he still wanted, the boy backed off several meters from the dead birds and stood with outstretched and open hands . . . waiting, waiting until the man came and placed the birds in his hands. He had, despite hunger, fear, and intense need, refused to take the birds. He waited until they were given to him; he received them.

That simple story summarizes all of Christ's moral teachings and the entire Ten Commandments. It is also a poignant illustration of chastity. If we, like this boy, would always wait until life was given to us as gift, as opposed to taking it as by right, seizing it, or raping it, we would never break a single commandment. Moreover, we would have in our lives the first, and most important, religious virtue of all, the sense that all is gift, that nothing is owed us by right.

In a way, this story is the opposite of the original sin story. In the Adam and Eve story, God gives them life and then adds a commandment which, on the surface, appears rather strange and arbitrary: "Do not eat of the fruit of the tree of knowledge and good and evil." What is this commandment?

In essence, what God is telling Adam and Eve is . . . "I am going to give you life. You may only receive that life. You may never take it. To take it is to ruin and destroy the gift that it is." Adam and Eve's sin was, ultimately, one of rape, the act of robbing, despoiling, and taking by force something that can only be had when it is received gratefully and respectfully as gift. Their sin, as is all sin, was an irreverence, the failure to respect the deepest foundations of a reality that is love contoured.

Simply put, the original sin was a failure in gratitude and receptivity, the failure to respect gift. It is no accident that the author of the story employs images (nakedness, shame) that are suggestive of sexual violation. That is the very point of the story, except that the rape that is being talked about here is wider than sex. In turning away from the posture of receptivity to the posture of seizing, Adam and Eve began to take by force, as by right, what was theirs only as gift. The result of that is always shame, a darkened mind, rationalization, and the beginnings of a dysfunctional world.

In the story of the boy who refused to take the very food he needed to live on, we see what the opposite of original sin looks like. That kind of patient, receptive waiting and respect might aptly be termed "original virtue" . . . and it is so needed today!

In a world whose spirit defines morality by achievement and the accumulation of things, and which invites us to demand our rights and suggests that "God helps those who help themselves," it is radically countercultural to suggest that patiently waiting to be given life (even when we are hungry) is better than actively seizing it.

To Adam and Eve, God said: "It is good, but it is gift—respect it as such. Don't ever take the apple!" All of morality is still summarized in that line. So is the essence of chastity.

CHAPTER 15

Chastity and Pornography

Pornography is the biggest addiction in the world today, and by a wide margin. Mostly it afflicts men, but it is also a growing addiction among women. Much of this of course is driven by its easy and free availability on the internet. Everyone now (not least our own young children) has immediate access to it from the privacy of their phones or laptops, and in anonymity. No more having to sneak off to some seedy section of the city to watch the forbidden. Today pornography is gaining more mainstream acceptance. What's the harm or shame in it?

Indeed, what's the harm or shame in it? For a growing number of people today there is no harm or shame in it. Their view is that whatever its downside, pornography is a liberation from former religious sexual repression. Indeed, many people see it as a healthy expression of sexuality (surprisingly, this includes even some feminist writers). Characters on mainstream television joke about their pornography collection as if it were as innocent as a collection of favorite old albums, and I have colleagues who argue that our resistance to it simply betrays sexual repression. Sex is beautiful, they argue, so why are we afraid to look at it?

What's wrong with pornography? Most everything, and not just from a moral perspective.

Let's begin with the argument: Sex is beautiful, so why are we afraid to look at it? That logic is right about one thing, sex is beautiful, so beautiful in fact that it needs to be protected from its own power. To say that it can be looked at as one might gaze at a beautiful sunset is naïve, religiously and psychologically. Religiously, we are told no one can look at God and live. That's also true for sex. Its very luminosity needs shrouding. Moreover, it's psychologically naïve to argue that this kind of deep intimacy can be put on public display. It can't and it shouldn't. Public display of that kind of intimacy violates all laws of propriety and respect for those engaged in this intimacy and those looking on. Like all things deeply intimate, it needs proper shrouding.

Next, when talking about the beauty of sex and the human body, we need to make a distinction between nudity and nakedness. When a good artist paints a nude body, the nudity serves to highlight the beauty of the whole person, body and soul, including his or her sexuality. In a nude painting, sexuality is connected to wholeness, to soul; how much to the contrary with nakedness. Nakedness exposes the human body in a way that obliterates its integrity, detaches its soul, and splits off sex from one's whole person. When this happens, and that is precisely what happens in pornography, sex becomes something soulless, split off, mechanical, devoid of deep meaning, bipolar, something from which you need to return to your real self. And,

when that happens, all profundity disappears and then, as
W. H. Auden writes, we all know the few things that we, as
mammals, can do.

Sadly, today for many of our young people, especially for
boys, pornography is their initial sex education, and it is one
that can leave a permanent imprint in them. That imprint
can have long-term effects in the way they understand the
meaning of sex, how they respect or disrespect women, and
how they grasp or don't grasp the vital soulful link between
sex and love. Pornography, and not just in the young, can
leave scars that are hard to overcome. The argument against
this is that pornography might well initially deform the
vision of an adolescent, but that this will be cured once
he matures and truly falls in love. My hope is that this is
true, but my worry is that the initial imprint can, long term,
taint the way a person falls in love and especially how he
understands the radical mutuality asked for of sex within
love. Such is the potential power of pornography.

Beyond all this, a strong argument might be made that
pornography (in its production and its viewing) is violence
against women, and that pornography subtly and not-so-
subtly promotes violence against women.

Finally, in a culture that prides itself above all else on its
sophistication and liberation, not least on its liberation from
many of our former religious taboos, one hesitates to even
mention the word "chastity" in this context. Dare one even
say that pornography is bad because it is the very antithesis
of chastity? Dare one use chastity as an argument when for

the most part our culture disdains chastity, pities it, and reserves a particular cynicism for religious groups who still advocate the adage "save it for your partner in marriage"? Worse still is today's cynicism vis-à-vis the idea of remaining chaste for Jesus. But the ideal of chastity embeds sex within romance, sacredness, commitment, community, and soul, whereas pornography portrays it as soulless and embeds it in a sick privacy. So, I leave you with the question: which one makes sex something dirty?

PART THREE

Carrying and Mourning Our Unfinished Symphony

"Our life is a short time in expectation, a time in which sadness and joy kiss each other at every moment. There is a quality of sadness that pervades all the moments of our life. It seems that there is no such thing as a clear-cut pure joy, but that even in the most happy moments of our existence we sense a tinge of sadness. In every satisfaction, there is an awareness of limitations. In every success, there is the fear of jealousy. Behind every smile, there is a tear. In every embrace, there is loneliness. In every friendship, distance. And in all forms of light, there is the knowledge of surrounding darkness. But this intimate experience in which every bit of life is touched by a bit of death can point us beyond the limits of our existence. It can do so by making us look forward in expectation to that day when our hearts will be filled with perfect joy, a joy that no one shall take away from us."

CHAPTER 16

The Torment of the Insufficiency of Everything Attainable

Novelist Anita Brookner suggests that in marriage, the first duty of each partner is to *"console the other for the fact that we cannot not disappoint each other."*

This isn't just a comment on marriage, but on life in general, where, sadly, our fantasy of finding some *"messiah"* to take away all our loneliness tends to be precisely what makes us too restless to remain happily inside our commitments, including marriage.

St. Augustine began his autobiography with the now-famous line: *"You have made us for yourself, Lord, and our hearts are restless until they rest in you!"* Thomas Aquinas taught that *"every choice is a renunciation,"* and that is why commitment, particularly a life-long commitment in marriage, is so difficult. Karl Rahner famously stated: *"In the torment of the insufficiency of everything attainable, we finally learn that here in this life all symphonies must remain unfinished."*

What each of these captures, in essence, is that in this life there is no such thing as clear-cut pure joy, and that we will live more peacefully and happily if we can accept that and not put false pressure on life, on our loved ones, and on God, to give us the full symphony right now.

Every day of their lives my parents prayed words to the effect that, this side of eternity, they were *"mourning and weeping in a valley of tears."* This didn't make them sad, morbid, or stoic. The opposite: it gave them the tools that they needed to accept life's real limits and the real limits and imperfections within community, church, family, and marriage. They were happier for knowing and accepting that.

My worry is that today we aren't equipping our own children in the same way. Instead, too often, we are helping them nurse the false expectation that, if they do it right, they can have it all in this life. All that is needed is to have the right body, the right career, the right city, the right neighborhood, the right friends, the right vacations, and the right soulmate, and they can have the full symphony here and now.

It's not to be had, and Anita Brookner's maxim that in marriage we *"cannot not disappoint each other"* simply states, in secular language, that no one, no matter how good, can be God for somebody else—and we will be happier if we understand that.

CHAPTER 17

Mourning Our Inconsummation

I n the Jewish Scriptures there's a story that's unique both in its capacity to shock and to fascinate. A king, Jephthah, is at war, and things are going badly. Praying in desperation, he makes a promise to God that, should he win this battle, he will, upon returning home, sacrifice on the altar the first person he meets.

Some days God has nothing better to do than to hear such prayers. Jephthah's prayer is granted and he wins the battle, but, upon returning home, he is deeply distressed because the first person he meets is his own daughter, in the full bloom of youth. He loves her deeply, grieves his foolish vow, and is ready to break it for her sake.

But she asks him to go ahead with it. She accepts to die on the altar of sacrifice, except for one thing (in stories that bare the soul there is always "one thing"). In her case, the one thing is this: she will now die a virgin, unconsummated, unfulfilled, not having achieved full intimacy, and not having given birth to children. And so she asks her father for time in the desert (forty days, the time it takes the desert to do its work) before she dies, to grieve her virginity, the incompleteness of her life.

Her father grants her wish, and she goes out into the desert with her companions (themselves virgins) for forty days to bewail that she will die a virgin. After this, she returns and is ready to die on the altar of sacrifice.

There's a rather nasty patriarchal character to this story (such were the times) and, of course, we are right to abhor the very idea of human sacrifice, but this particular story is not historical and is not meant literally. It's archetypal, a metaphor, a poetry of the soul within which death and virginity are not meant in their literal sense. What do death and virginity mean in this story?

They're metaphors inside a parable meant to teach a profound truth, namely, all of us, no matter our age or state in life, must, at some point, mourn what's incomplete and not consummated in our lives.

We are all Jephthah's daughters. In the end, like her, we all die virgins, having lived incomplete lives, not having achieved the intimacy we craved, and having yearned to create a lot more things than we were able to birth. In this life, nobody gets the full symphony. There's a place inside us where we all "bewail our virginity," and this is true too of married people, just as it is of celibates. At some deep level, this side of eternity, we all sleep alone.

We need to mourn this, whatever form that might take. When we fail to do this, we go through life disappointed, dissatisfied with our lives, restless inside our own skins, prone to anger, and forever expecting, unrealistically, that someone or something—a marriage partner, a family, a child, a church, a sexual partner, a friend, a career, or an achievement—can take all our loneliness away, give us the complete symphony, and (metaphorically) consummate our lives so that we aren't virgins anymore.

Of course that's impossible: only God can do that. Our yearnings and our needs are infinite because we are Grand Canyons without a bottom. For that reason, we all sleep alone, living (as Rahner famously puts it) in the torment of the insufficiency of everything attainable.

Recognizing and accepting this isn't one of our strengths. Most everything in our culture today conspires to keep us from admitting this. No more for us the old prayer, "To thee we send up our sighs, mourning and weeping in this valley of tears." Good for past generations, but not for us. The last thing we like to admit is tears, the helpless frustration of our lives at times, and the incontrovertible fact of our own virginity.

We suffer a lot of restlessness, disappointment, and bitterness because of this. Until, like Jephthah's daughter, we can recognize and admit and honor how we really feel, we will forever be fighting something or somebody—usually those persons and things closest to us.

The daydreams of our youth eventually die, though perhaps as we get older we replay them just to feel old sentiments (our own version of *The Way We Were*) rather than with any kind of practical hope. Time and disappointment have done their work; we no longer look for the daydreams to come true, and the dreams themselves look flat in the context of our actual lives. But what created those dreams all those years back hasn't changed; indeed, there's a part of us now that's more idealistic than before, and we ache just as much as we ever did, even now when we accept that daydreams don't come true.

When that happens, it's time to go into the desert and bewail our virginity. Our capacity for genuine self-sacrifice, it would seem, follows from that.

CHAPTER 18

Carrying Tension as a Gift to Others

What a mature adult is asked to do for his or her family and community is to carry, absorb, and transform the tension that's there. This is also the penultimate invitation within adult discipleship. This is what the Gospels call "pondering."

In the Gospels this is used, first of all, to describe what Mary, the mother of Jesus, was forced to do at some moments in her life. The Gospels tell us simply that Mary "pondered" these things in her heart. What is meant by that?

Sometimes our English translations translate this from its original Greek with the word "treasured," implying that Mary was careful to truly remember what happened at that moment. That, no doubt, is part of its meaning. But there is more.

To understand what it means to ponder in the biblical sense we need to make a key distinction: One can ponder in the Greek sense and one can ponder in the Hebrew sense. Pondering in the Greek sense might aptly be defined by an expression that comes to us from Greek philosophy: *The unexamined life is not worth living.* Our commonsense notion is very much tied to that notion of pondering, where to ponder means to try to think something through in all its depth and implications. One pictures, for example, Rodin's famous sculpture of the thinker, someone sitting in a chapel or on a mountainside, intensely reflecting on something, mulling it over, considering all its various angles. But this would be what the word would mean had the Gospels been written by Aristotle.

But the Gospels, while written in Greek, are Hebrew in thought, and there, pondering has a different, more existential connotation. Simply put, to ponder, in the Hebrew sense, meant *to hold, carry, and transform tension so as not to give it back in kind, knowing that whatever energies we do not transform we will transmit.*

This can be understood more clearly by looking at its opposite. In the Gospels, the opposite of pondering is not to "not ponder," but to "be amazed." Notice in the Gospels how often a crowd is described as reacting to something Jesus said or did with the words "and they were amazed." Jesus is rarely happy with this reaction. It is in essence a "mindless" reaction, where a crowd simply lets an energy flow through it. Crowds tend to do that—and so do we.

With an apology that these images are more mechanical than soulful, allow me to contrast the biblical image of "pondering" with the biblical image of "amazement." An image for amazement is that of an electrical wire; it simply lets the energy flow through it. One hundred and twenty volts in—one hundred and twenty volts out. An image for "pondering" is that of a water purifier. A water purifier does not simply let things flow through it. It takes in contaminated water, water filled with toxins, dirt, impurities, and poisons, and it holds those contaminates inside itself and gives out just the pure water. That's the biblical image of "pondering," and the invitation to do that is the penultimate invitation within Christian discipleship and the penultimate invitation vis-à-vis coming to human maturity.

How does this relate to chastity? In an obvious way. We are always living with tension. Inside that tension, do we ponder or are we amazed? Are we water purifiers transforming tension or are we electrical wires that simply let tension flow out through us no matter the consequences for others or for ourselves? Do we hold, carry, and transform tension so as to live with the reverence, respect, and patience love demands? Or do we violate the natural unfolding of a moth coming out of its cocoon because of the impatience innate in our tension? Clearly too, this is particularly true regarding how we deal with sexual tension in our lives.

CHAPTER 19

An Invitation to Metanoia

In 1986, Czechoslovakian novelist Ivan Klima published a series of autobiographical essays entitled *My First Loves*. These essays describe some of his moral struggles as a young agnostic seeking answers without any explicit moral framework within which to frame those struggles. He's a young man, full of sexual passion, but hesitant to act out sexually, even as all his peers, men and women, seemingly do not share that same reticence. He remains celibate, but isn't sure why; certainly it's not for religious reasons, since he's agnostic. Why is he living as he is? Is he being responsible or is he simply uptight and lacking in nerve?

He's unsure and so he asks himself: if I died and there is a God and I met that God, what would God say to me? Would God chastise me for being uptight or would God praise me for carrying my solitude at a high level? Would God look at me with disappointment or would he congratulate me for honoring my soul?

As he writes this book, Klima doesn't know the answer to that question. He's not sure what God would say to him and whether at any given moment God is smiling or frowning upon him. Irrespective of the answer, what's insightful here I believe, is how Klima frames his moral choice. For him, it's not a question of what's sinful or not, but rather a question of carrying his solitude and tension in a way that makes for nobility of soul.

At first glance, of course, that can seem self-serving; trying to be special can also make for a pride that's very judgmental. However, true nobility of soul isn't something sought for its own sake but something sought for the good of others and to properly honor one's own nature. One does not try to be good to set oneself apart from others. Rather one tries to be good in order to create a beacon of stability, respect, hospitality, and chastity for others.

This, I believe, can be a second starting point for spirituality as this pertains to morality, to what's right or wrong in our lives. The first starting point, of course, is more basic. It focuses on keeping the Ten Commandments, and most of these begin with a negative warning, "thou shalt not." At a base level, morality has been very much identified with ethics, with sorting out what's right and what's wrong, what's sinful and what's not. However, keeping the Ten Commandments and sorting out what's a sin and what's not, while critically important, is to morality what elementary arithmetic is to higher mathematics: a necessary base, no more. Once that fundamental base has been essentially achieved, the real task starts, namely the struggle to become bighearted, to put on the heart of Christ, to become a saint so as to create a better world for others.

Let me risk an earthy example to try to illustrate this. When I was a seminarian studying moral theology, one day in class we were examining various questions of sexual morality. At one point, the question arose as to the sinfulness or non-sinfulness of masturbation. Is this an intrinsic disorder? Seriously sinful or nothing serious? What's to be said morally about this question?

After weighing the various opinions of students, the professor said this: I don't think the important question is whether this is a sin or not. There's a better way of framing this. Here's where I land on this question: I disagree with those who say it's a serious sin, but I also disagree with those who see no moral issue here whatsoever. The issue here is not so much whether this is a sin or not; rather, it's a question of at what level, compensatory or heroic, we want to carry this tension. In the face of this issue, I need to ask myself, at what level do I want to carry my solitude? How noble of soul can I be? How much can I accept to carry this tension to make for a more chaste community inside the body of Christ?

At this second level, living a moral life ceases being a command and becomes an invitation, to have a greater nobility of soul for the sake of the world. Can I be more bighearted? Can I be less petty? Can I carry more tension without giving in to compensation? Can I be more forgiving? Can I love a person from whom I'm separated by temperament and ideology? Can I be a saint? Saints don't think so much in terms of what's sinful and what isn't. Rather they ask, what is the more loving thing to do here?

What's more noble of soul and what's more petty? What serves the world better?

In the Synoptic Gospels, the first word out of Jesus' mouth is the word *Metanoia*, a word that implies infinitely more than what's connoted in its English translation, *Repent*. Metanoia is a combination of two Greek words, *Meta* (above) and *Nous* (mind). It is also the antithesis of *paranoia*. Metanoia is an invitation to put on a higher mind, to be more noble of heart, and to leave paranoia, pettiness, and self-gratification behind.

That is also the invitation that lies inside the concept of chastity. Inside all the tension I feel within life, sexual and other, can I carry my solitude at a level that stands before others and the world with proper reverence, respect, and patience?

PART FOUR

Some Personal Reflections

"I smile before my impossible resolution to chastity. It is up to you [Lord] to realize it in my weakness, which I wish to be humble, submissive, courageous. To love chastity. To want this freedom for your Love in me, for your salvation working through me here. To pray for your enemies (for love of you) is something that partakes of the chastity of the heart that is purified by the desire of the salvation of all, a heart that is detached, ungrasping, surrendered. . . . Chastity becomes a weapon of non-violence in the context of enemies and persecutions; it becomes an opening of the heart stronger than the withdrawal into oneself proper to the egotistical and narcissistic affect."

Maybe I will never have children of my own . . . it may be that my children will always be temporary, never to be held. But so are everyone's.

CHAPTER 20

Chastity and Celibacy–A Personal Apologia

As a Roman Catholic priest and a vowed religious celibate, I'm very conscious that today celibacy, whether lived out in a religious commitment or in other circumstances, is suspect, under siege, and is offering too little by way of a helpful apologia to its critics. Is there a value in choosing celibacy for religious reasons? The only real answer I can give comes from my own life.

What's my response to a culture that, for the most part, believes celibacy is both a naïveté and a dualism that stands against the goodness of sexuality, renders its adherents less than fully human, and lies at the root of the clerical sexual abuse crisis within the Roman Catholic Church? What might I say in its defense?

First, that celibacy isn't a basis for pedophilia? Virtually all empirical studies indicate that pedophilia is a diagnosis not linked to celibacy. But then let me acknowledge celibacy's downside: celibacy is not the normal state for anyone. When God made the first man and woman, God said: "It is not good for the human being to be alone." That isn't just a statement about the constitutive place of community within our lives (though it is that); it's a clear reference to sexuality, its fundamental goodness, and its God-intended place in our lives. From that, it flows that to be a celibate, particularly to choose to be one, comes fraught with real dangers.

Celibacy can, and sometimes does, lead to an unhealthy sense of one's sexual and relational self and to a coldness that's often judgmental. It can too, understandably, lead to an unhealthy sexual preoccupation within the celibate. Moreover, in its clerical expression, it provides access to certain forms of intimacy within which a dangerous betrayal of trust can occur.

Less recognized, but a huge danger, is that it can be a vehicle for selfishness. Simply put, without the conscriptive demands that come with marriage and child-raising, there's the ever-present danger that a celibate can, unconsciously, arrange his life too much to suit his own needs.

Thus celibacy is not for everyone; indeed, it's not for the many. It contains an inherent abnormality. Consecrated celibacy is not simply a different lifestyle, it's an anomaly. As Thomas Merton, speaking of his own celibacy, once said: *The absence of woman is a fault in my chastity*; but that can have its own rich purpose and contain its own potential for generativity.

As well, I believe that consecrated celibacy, like music or religion, needs to be judged by its best expressions and not by its aberrations. Celibacy should not be judged by those who have not given it a wholesome expression but by the many wonderful women and men, saints of the past and present, who have given it a wholesome and generative expression.

One could name numerous saints of the past or wonderfully healthy and generative persons from our own generation as examples where vowed celibacy has made for a wholesome, happy life that inspires others: Mother Teresa, Oscar Romero, Raymond E. Brown, and Helen Prejean, to name just a few. Personally, I know many very generative, vowed celibates whose wholesomeness I envy and who make celibacy credible—and attractive.

Like marriage, though in a different way, celibacy offers a rich potential for intimacy and generativity. As a vowed celibate I am grateful for a vocation that has brought me intimately into the world of so many people.

When I left home at a young age to enter the Missionary Oblates of Mary Immaculate, I confess, I didn't want celibacy. Nobody should. I wanted to be a missionary and a priest, but celibacy presented itself as the stumbling block. Once inside religious life, almost immediately, I loved the life, though not the celibacy part. Twice I delayed taking final vows, unsure about celibacy.

Eventually I made the decision, a hard leap of trust, and took the vow for life. Full disclosure, celibacy has been for me singularly the hardest part of my more than fifty years in religious life . . . but, but, at the same time, it has helped create a special kind of entry into the world and into others' lives that is a precious grace I pray I will never betray.

The natural God-given desire for sexual intimacy, for exclusivity in affection, for the marriage bed, for children, for grandchildren, doesn't leave you, and it shouldn't. But celibacy has helped bring into my life a rich, consistent, deep intimacy. Reflecting on my celibate vocation, all I may legitimately feel is gratitude.

Celibacy isn't for everyone. It excludes you from the normal; it seems brutally unfair at times; it's fraught with dangers ranging from serious betrayal of trust to living a selfish life; and it's a fault in one's very chastity—but, if lived out in fidelity, it can be wonderfully generative and does not exclude you from either real intimacy or real happiness.

CHAPTER 21

Sex, Chastity, and My Mother's Little Pamphlets

I learned about the birds and the bees on the playground in my early years in middle school. A boy slightly older than the rest of us sat us down one day and gave us the talk that our parents hadn't given us. His facts weren't totally accurate, but they were accurate enough to give us the basics, and these were enough to begin the process of awakening in me a series of dark, inchoate feelings. My childhood was over; adolescence had begun.

But the talk from my parents about the birds and the bees was still to come, and it rescued me from an image of sex that too often stays with us when we've learned about sex from immature peers on the playground. And, for me, that talk did not come from my father, it came from my mother. Moreover, it didn't come in the form of talk: *Sit down, there's something important we need to talk about*. It came in the form of a little religious pamphlet that my mother had picked up at our church or from the nuns who taught us catechism during summer vacation.

This was more than sixty years ago, and the devotional literature in Roman Catholic circles then wasn't particularly sophisticated psychologically. But this little pamphlet, for all its piety, psychological simplicity, and stumbling language that couldn't quite use the biological words and talked awkwardly of "wet dreams," got something deeply right and imprinted that indelibly into my soul. It taught me that the first thing we need to say about sex is that it is holy, a sacred gift, a sacred trust, the most soulful thing in life, and that it is a beautiful thing that needs to be honored, protected, and never violated. And, to imprint this into our romantic imagination, this little pamphlet shared stories of saints (like Maria Goretti) who chose to die rather than to compromise the sacredness of their sexuality. Sexual integrity, it told us, was worth dying for.

Today that may sound pious, simplistic, and overly idealistic, but it cured me, and permanently, from all notions that sex is dirty, secretive, something to happen under the cover of darkness, and something that sets you against spirituality, religion, and God. Sex is sacred. It is God-given and it does not set you against spirit. When one believes this, chastity is a natural consequence. I went through adolescence and into early adulthood with that understanding of sex ruling over all else, including the tumultuous sexual pressures that assail us during those years.

However, the real test vis-à-vis this notion came once I had graduated from the seclusion and protection of my seminary years, entered the ministry, and began again to live within the full sexual winds of our culture. I found myself, and this, my childhood notion of sex, to be largely out of step with most everything. More and more, in my ministry and with the friends and colleagues whom I was with in various graduate schools, I found myself to be part of an ever-shrinking minority. For them, sex was understood to be something casual, or at least one could make it so.

I remember a workshop I once led for a group of young adults where I was trying to instill the idea that sex is something soulful and sacred, and a young woman challenged me to this effect: "Sex is only something sacred if you make it so. It can be sacred, but it can also be something casual, not connected to anything deep or permanent inside us. *Sex is what you make it*—sacred or casual." This woman was in her early twenties, not yet looking for a marriage partner and enjoying her freedom. It would be interesting to see if she would say the same thing as a wife and mother, thirty or forty years later.

Some years ago, Reginald Bibby, Canada's leading sociologist of religion, did an extensive study of the religious attitudes and behaviors of the millennial generation. What he found in terms of their attitude towards sex and marriage is interesting. On the one hand, the majority of them want eventually to find a life partner and end up in a monogamous marriage. This is the endgame vis-à-vis how they understand the intentionality of their sexuality. They want the marriage bed—and most often too, want a wedding in white. However, many believe they can first have several years to experience sex without it being connected to commitment and soul. The idea (perhaps more unconscious than conscious) is that they can go through a period of their lives wherein sex is casual and not connected to soul, and then at a given time when one has met the right person and is ready for permanent commitment, one can sacralize his or her sex and make it holy. Sex can be casual and non-soulful, until one makes it sacred and soulful.

Will this work? Is sexuality that malleable in its essence? For some, with the grace of God, it will work. And I am grateful for that. However, if fifty years of ministry and dealing with peoples' lives has taught me anything, it has taught me that the little catechetical pamphlet my mother gave me all those years ago is right. Sex is inextricably linked to soul. It is sacred. It cannot be altered to make it mean anything you want it to mean.

And chastity follows from that, naturally and necessarily.

CHAPTER 22

Celibacy in a Post-Modern World

Cardinal Francis George was once asked what he thought of the radical pacifism of people like Dorothy Day and Daniel Berrigan, prophetic figures who believed in absolute nonviolence.

He was asked, "How can this be practical?" ; it's utterly naïve to believe that we can live without police and without soldiers. This was his reply: *The world needs pacifists in the same way as it needs vowed celibates:* they're not practical. They're out of place in this world. But they point to the eschatological world, the world of heaven, a world within which there will be no guns, where relational exclusivities will not exist as they exist now, where family will not be based on biology, blood, or marriage, where there will be no poor people, and where everything will belong to everyone.

I thought of that recently as I was conducting a workshop on religious life for a group of young people who were discerning whether to enter vowed religious life. My task was not to try to persuade them to join a religious community but to help them understand what that life, should they join it, would entail. That meant, of course, long discussions on the value or non-value of celibacy.

What's to be said about celibacy in a world that for the most part identifies celibacy as frigidity?

Well, no doubt, celibacy is seen as radically countercultural, and it is. But that might in fact speak to its prophetic value. Celibacy, properly understood, is not a missing out on the joys of sexuality. It's a rich modality of sexuality itself, given that being sexual means more than having sex. Sexuality is a beautiful, God-given drive within us for community, friendship, togetherness, wholeness, family, play, altruism, enjoyment, delight, creativity, genital consummation, and for everything that takes us beyond our aloneness and makes us generative. The very real joys that are found in community, friendship, and service of others are not a second-rate substitute for sex. They bring their own sexual flourishing in terms of leading us out of our aloneness. Living a celibate life is not a renunciation of sexuality. Lived properly, it can be a rich modality of sex itself.

But, our thoughts and our feelings are strongly influenced by the cultural software within which we find ourselves. Thus, given how our culture understands sex today, this may well be the most difficult time in many centuries to choose to make a religious vow of celibacy and live that out.

Small wonder religious communities are not overflooded with applications. However, because it is more difficult than ever, it is perhaps more important than ever that a number of women and men choose, voluntarily, to make a vow that points to the fact that in heaven there will be no guns, relational exclusivities will not exist as they exist now, family will not be based on biology, blood, or marriage, there will be no poor people, and everything will belong to everyone.

PART FIVE

Chastity Without a Cringe

"There's only one real sin, and that is to persuade oneself that second-best is anything but the second-best."

—*Doris Lessing*

"The bird's beauty comes out most when the wind opposes it."

—*G. M. Hopkins*

CHAPTER 23

Wonder Has Left the Building

In a poem entitled "Is/Not," Margaret Atwood suggests that when a love grows numb, this is where we find ourselves:

> We're stuck here
> on this side of the border
> in this country of thumbed streets and stale
>   buildings
>
> where there is nothing spectacular to see
> and the weather is ordinary
>
> where love occurs in its pure form only
> on the cheaper of the souvenirs

Love can grow numb between two people, just as it can within a whole culture. And that has happened in our culture, at least to a large part. The excitement that once guided our eyes has given way to a certain numbness and resignation. We no longer stand before life with much freshness. We have seen what it has to offer and have succumbed to a certain resignation: *That's all there is, and it's not that great!* All we can try for now is more of the same, with the misguided hope that if we keep increasing the dosage the payoff will be better.

They talk of old souls, but old souls are actually young at heart. We are the opposite, young souls no longer young at heart. Wonder has left the building.

What's at the root of this? What has deprived us of wonder? Familiarity and its children: sophistication, intellectual pride, disappointment, boredom, and contempt. *Familiarity does breed contempt*, and contempt is the antithesis of the two things needed to stand before the world in wonder—reverence and respect.

G. K. Chesterton once suggested that *familiarity is the greatest of all illusions*. Elizabeth Barrett Browning gives poetic expression to this:

> *Earth's crammed with heaven.*
> *And every common bush afire with God.*
> *But only he who sees, takes off his shoes.*
> *The rest sit round and pluck blackberries,*
> *   and daub their natural faces unaware.*

That aptly describes the illusion of familiarity: plucking berries while carelessly stroking our faces, unaware that we are in the presence of the holy. Familiarity renders all things common.

What's the answer? How do we recover our sense of wonder? How do we begin again to see divine fire inside ordinary life? Chesterton suggests that the secret to recovering wonder and seeing divine fire in the ordinary is to *learn to look at things familiar until they look unfamiliar again*. Biblically, that's what God asks of Moses when Moses sees a burning bush in the desert and approaches its fire out of curiosity. God says to him, *Take off your shoes, the ground you are standing on is holy ground.*

That single line, that singular invitation, is the deep secret to recover our sense of wonder whenever we find ourselves, as Atwood describes, stuck on this side of the border, in thumbed streets and stale buildings, with nothing spectacular to see, ordinary weather, and love seemingly cheapened everywhere.

Oliver Wendell Holmes once wrote, "I wouldn't give a fig for the simplicity on this side of complexity. But I'd give my life for the simplicity on the other side of complexity."

Our sense of wonder is predicated initially on the naïveté of being a child, of not yet being unhealthily familiar with the world. Our eyes then are still open to marvel at the newness of things. Of course that changes as we grow, experience life, and learn. Soon enough we learn the truth about Santa and the Easter Bunny, and with that, all too easily, comes the death of wonder and the familiarity that breeds contempt.

This is a disillusionment which, while a normal transitional phase in life, is not meant to be a place where we stay. The task of adulthood is to regain our sense of wonder and begin again, for very different reasons, to believe in the reality of Santa and the Easter Bunny. We need to bring wonder back into the building.

I once heard a wise man share this vignette: imagine a two-year-old child who asks you, "Where does the sun go at night?" For a child that young, don't pull out a globe or a book and try to explain how the solar system works. Just tell the child the sun is tired and is taking a sleep behind the barn. However, when the child is six or seven years old, don't try that anymore. Then, it's time to pull out books and explain the solar system. After that, when the child is in high school or college, it's time to pull out Steven Hawking, Brian Swimme, and astrophysicists, and talk about the origins and makeup of the universe. Finally, when the person is eighty years old, it's enough again to say, the sun is tired and is taking a sleep behind the barn.

We have grown too familiar with sunsets! Wonder can make the familiar unfamiliar again, and there is no wonder unless there is chastity.

CHAPTER 24

Chastity without a Cringe

This book began with the question, *"Can purity be a word that is ever used without a cringe?"* For many, perhaps for most people in our culture today, these words cannot be used without a cringe. The concepts of sexual purity and chastity have fallen on hard times today. At least, so it would seem at first glance. Our culture prides itself on being liberated and tends to see the ideals of sexual purity and chastity as repressive holdovers from the past and blames the churches for giving us guilt complexes around the issue of sex.

But that is only half of what is happening. Even while chastity is disappearing out one door, it is reappearing in another guise through another door. Freud said that sometimes we understand things more clearly when we see them fractured, and that is the case here. We are beginning to see more clearly the importance of chastity in the consequences we see when it is ignored and broken.

I once heard a renowned theologian say this to an auditorium full of people. As a woman and a feminist, she nursed some grievances vis-à-vis how the churches have treated women, gender, and sexuality. At one point she focused on the sexuality aspect and made this bold statement: *"The church has never had a healthy, robust theology and spirituality of sex. It has been timid, rigid, Manichean, and simply hung up on sex. It's been afraid of sex."* So far, so good—there's truth in this. But then she asked this: *"Why is the church so afraid of sex? Who has been hurt by it anyway?"*

Wow! The better question, I believe, would be, "Who hasn't been hurt by it?" Every day and everywhere we are witness to heartbreak, to depression, to murders, to suicides, and to breakdowns of all sorts as a result of sex—betrayal, infidelity, jealousy, obsession, anger.

Freud is right. Sometimes we understand the structure of a thing more clearly when we see it broken. That, I submit, is very apropos regarding chastity. Today, more clearly than ever before, we are realizing how deeply a soul is wounded as a result of sexual abuse, rape, and sexual harassment. These are the antitheses of chastity, and we see their devastating effects. It is not only for religious reasons that so many women throughout history have chosen to die rather than to submit to sexual victimization. The same holds true vis-à-vis gender equality. Without a healthy chastity (reverence, respect, and patience) in our relationships there will be little progress on the road to sexual and gender justice.

Kerry Robinson defines a cynic as someone who has given up, but not shut up! This, I believe, is true of most of the bitter critics of chastity today. They are cynical, but they radiate a deep fatigue and pessimism. And pessimism, as G. K. Chesterton once said, is not being tired of the evil, but being tired of the good. Soul fatigue does not lie in being weary of suffering, but in being weary of joy. Our culture today, for all its sophistication, suffers from a certain fatigue of the soul. There's pleasure, but there's precious little genuine delight. Joy has also left the building. And that's not surprising. A culture that's short on chastity is also short on joy.

The French novelist Leon Bloy once wrote that *ultimately there is only one true sadness, that of not being a saint*. To which one might add this comment from Simone Weil: *Today it's not enough to be merely a saint; rather we must have the saintliness demanded by the present moment.*

What's needed today are more erotic, chaste, joy-filled persons who can say the word *chastity* without a cringe.

ACKNOWLEDGEMENTS

No book is the product of just one person. I need to express thanks to a lot of people for their help in bringing this book to birth.

First, a huge thanks to Paraclete Press, to Rachel McKendree and others who invited me to write this book and gently kept prodding me as deadlines were missed.

Thanks also to JoAnne Chrones, my Executive Assistant, who for more than twenty-five years has helped keep me afloat, and today keeps me from drowning in the sea of social media and over-extension.

A special thanks to Doug Mitchell who, when he isn't composing folk songs or on tour, generously takes time to lay hawk's eye to my writings and teach me the grammar I should have learned in high school.

Thanks to my four families: The community here at Oblate School of Theology in San Antonio, Texas, who support me always, are my Eucharist community and my intellectual stimulus. Next, the religious community of which I am a member, the *Missionary Oblates of Mary Immaculate*, who through more than fifty years have fed me, housed me, given me exceptional educational opportunities, and entrusted me with ministry. Then, not least, there is a large amorphous tribe of biological family scattered throughout Canada, who give me roots, gave me faith, taught me banter, and first taught me chastity. Finally, there are those who give me friendship, another amorphous tribe that keeps me sane and keeps me aware of what's important in life.

Finally, I want to thank you, the reader, for picking up this book. It's a note in a milk bottle sent floating out into the open sea, hoping someone marooned on an isolated island might find it. Thanks for picking it up.

A thousand thanks to all of you.

NOTES

CHAPTER ONE

v   ***Can purity be a word:*** Lisbeth During, *The Chastity Plot* (Chicago: University of Chicago Press, 2021), 303.

x   ***erotically lame:*** Allan Bloom, T*he Closing of the American Mind* (New York: Simon and Schuster, 1988).

3   ***Nikos Kazantzakis shares this story:*** Nikos Kazantzakis, *Zorba the Greek*, was originally published in Greek in 1946. There are now are dozens of editions and translations of this book in English. The incident referred to here appears in the last three paragraphs of Chapter X.

5   ***Albert Camus wrote:*** Olivier Todd, *Albert Camus, A Life* (New York, Knopf, 1997), 157.

7   ***Be patient! Learn to wait:*** This is not a direct quote but is, in essence, the whole message of Carlo Carretto's book *Letters from the Desert* (Maryknoll, NY: Orbis, 1972).

CHAPTER TWO

9   ***Chastity as Purity of Heart:*** Some material in this chapter appeared in Ron Rolheiser, "Chastity as Purity of Heart And Intention," January 15, 2011, https://ronrolheiser.com/chastity-as-purity-of-heart-and-intention-2/.

11   ***I am not trying to be condescending:*** Charles Taylor, *A Secular Age* (Cambridge, MA: Belknap Press of Harvard University, 2007), 767.

CHAPTER THREE

13n1   ***Chastity, Love, and Sex:*** Some material in this chapter appeared in Ron Rolheiser, "Chastity and Love," September 10, 2018, https://ronrolheiser.com/chastity-and-love/.

13n2   ***Woe to chastity that is not practiced:*** Benoit Standaert, *Spirituality: An Art of Living: A Monk's Alphabet of Spiritual Practices* (Minneapolis: Liturgical Press, 2018), 23.

CHAPTER FOUR

17   ***Chastity and Innocence:*** Some material in this chapter appeared in Ron Rolheiser, "Of Innocence, Purity and

Chastity," May 1, 2023, https://ronrolheiser.com/of-innocence-purity-and-chastity/.

18 *The church combats the passions:* Friedrich Nietzsche, quoted by Lisbeth During in The Chastity Plot, 131.

CHAPTER FIVE

21 *Sublimation and the Sublime:* Some material in this chapter appeared in Ron Rolheiser, "Advent: Preparing for the Sublime," November 26, 2000, https://ronrolheiser.com/advent-preparing-for-the-sublime/.

CHAPTER SIX

25 *The Goddess of Chastity:* The material in this chapter appeared in Ron Rolheiser, "The Goddess of Chastity," October 30, 2014, https://ronrolheiser.com/the-goddess-of-chastity/.

26 *Although she is the most virginal:* Thomas Moore, *The Soul of Sex: Cultivating Life as an Act of Love* (New York: HarperPerennial, 1999), 63–64.

CHAPTER SEVEN

29 *Chastity as Blessing Others:* Some material in this chapter appeared in Ron Rolheiser, "Blessing Others as the Endgame of Sexuality," June 5, 2023, https://ronrolheiser.com/blessing-others-as-the-endgame-of-sexuality/.

CHAPTER EIGHT

37 *A Plea for the Soul:* Some material in this chapter appeared in Ron Rolheiser, "A Plea for the Soul," October 30, 2017, https://ronrolheiser.com/a-plea-for-the-soul/.

40 *The Right to Sex:* Amia Srinivasan, *The Right to Sex* (New York: Farrar, Straus and Giroux, 2021).

CHAPTER NINE

43 *Our Dark Memory of Our Soul:* The material in this chapter appeared in Ron Rolheiser, "Dark Memory," November 12, 2006, https://ronrolheiser.com/dark-memory/.

CHAPTER TEN

47 *Sex and the Soul:* Some material in this chapter appeared

in Ron Rolheiser, "Listening to Our Souls," December 13, 2021,"https://ronrolheiser.com/listening-to-our-souls/.

48   ***Suicide and the Soul:*** James Hillman, *Suicide and the Soul* (New York: Spring Publications, 2020).

CHAPTER ELEVEN

51n1   ***Chastity as Soulful and Taking Us Home:*** Some material in this chapter appeared in Ron Rolheiser, "Where Is Home?", May 20, 2019, https://ronrolheiser.com/where-is-home/.

51n2   ***Only the Heart Knows How to Find Them:*** Christopher de Vinck, *Only the Heart Knows How to Find Them: Precious Memories for a Faithless Time* (New York: Viking, 1991).

CHAPTER TWELVE

55   ***The Closing of the American Mind:*** Allan Bloom, *The Closing of the American Mind* (New York: Simon & Schuster, 1987).

CHAPTER THIRTEEN

61   ***In a world bathed:*** Trevor Herriot, *The Road Is How: A Prairie Pilgrimage through Nature, Desire and Soul* (Toronto: Harper Collins, 2013), 129.

CHAPTER FOURTEEN

63   ***The Original Sin as a Failure in Chastity:*** Some material in this chapter appeared in Ron Rolheiser, "How Not to Commit the Original Sin," May 30, 1991, https://ronrolheiser.com/how-not-to-commit-the-original-sin/.

CHAPTER FIFTEEN

67   ***Chastity and Pornography:*** The material in this chapter appeared in Ron Rolheiser, "Pornography and Chastity," January 31, 2022, https://ronrolheiser.com/pornography-and-chastity/.

PART THREE:
CARRYING AND MOURNING OUR UNFINISHED SYMPHONY

71   ***Our life is a short time in expectation:*** Henri Nouwen, *Making All Things New: An Invitation to the Spiritual Life* (San Francisco: Harper & Row, 1981), 51-53.

CHAPTER SIXTEEN

73n1 **Novelist Anita Brookner suggests:** This a leitmotif in the novels of Anita Brookner. See, for example, her award-winning novel, *Brief Lives* (New York: Random House, 1991).

73n2 **In the torment of the insufficiency:** Karl Rahner, *Servants of the Lord* (New York, Herder and Herder, 1968), 152.

CHAPTER SEVENTEEN

75n1 **Mourning Our Inconsummation:** Some of the material in this chapter was used in Ron Rolheiser, "Mourning Our Inconsummation," January 20, 20022, https://ronrolheiser.com/mourning-our-inconsummation/.

75n2 **In the Jewish Scriptures there's a story:** The Book of Judges, chapter 11.

CHAPTER NINETEEN

83n1 **An Invitation to Metanoia:** Some of the material in this chapter appeared in Ron Rolheiser, "An Invitation to Something Higher," March 1, 2021, https://ronrolheiser.com/an-invitation-to-something-higher/.

83n2 **My First Loves:** Ivan Klíma, *My First Loves,* tr. Ewald Osers (New York: Harper & Row, 1988).

PART FOUR: SOME PERSONAL REFLECTIONS

87 **I smile before my impossible resolution:** From the Journals of Christophe Lebreton, OCSO, Monk of Tibhirine (Atlas), in *Born From the Gaze of God*, Monastic Wisdom Series, Vol. 37, tr. Mette Louise Nygård and Edith Scholl, OCSO (Collegeville, MN: Cistercian Publications, 2014), 143-44.

CHAPTER TWENTY

89 **Chastity and Celibacy – A Personal Apologia:** Some of the material in this chapter appeared in Ron Rolheiser, "Celibacy–A Personal Apologia," February 11, 2019, https://ronrolheiser.com/celibacy-a-personal-apologia/.

CHAPTER TWENTY-ONE

95 **Reginald Bibby … did an extensive study:** Reginald Bibby, *The Emerging Millennials: How Canada's Newest*

About Paraclete Press

Paraclete Press is the publishing arm of the Cape Cod Benedictine community, the Community of Jesus. Presenting a full expression of Christian belief and practice, we reflect the ecumenical charism of the Community and its dedication to sacred music, the fine arts, and the written word.

SCAN
TO
READ
MORE

www.paracletepress.com

You may also be interested in...

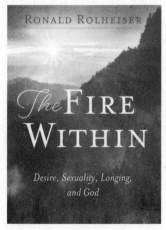

Generation Is Responding To Change & Choice (Kelowna, BC: Woodlake Books), 2009.

CHAPTER TWENTY-TWO

97 ***Celibacy in a Post-Modern World:*** Some of the material in this chapter appeared in Ron Rolheiser,"Poverty, Chastity, and Obedience in a Secular Age," April 30, 2018, https://ronrolheiser.com/poverty-chastity-and-obedience-in-a-secular-age/.

CHAPTER TWENTY-THREE

102n1 ***Wonder Has Left the Building:*** Some of the material in this chapter appeared in Ron Rolheiser, "Wonder Has Left the Building," https://ronrolheiser.com/wonder-has-left-the-building/.

102n2 ***We're stuck here:*** Margaret Atwood, "Is/Not." https://poemanalysis.com/margaret-atwood/is-not (London, UK: Poem Solutions Limited, 2023).

104n1 ***familiarity is the greatest of all illusions:*** G. K. Chesterton, *The Everlasting Man* (London, UK: Hodder & Stoughton, 1925), 159.

104n2 ***Earth's crammed with heaven:*** Elizabeth Barrett Browning,"Earth's crammed with heaven": onejourney.net/elizabeth-barrett-browning-quote-earth-is-crammed-with-heaven/ (Merlin, OR: Life of Learning Foundation, Inc., 2023).

105 ***Take off your shoes:*** Exodus 3.

CHAPTER TWENTY-FOUR

108 ***Kerry Robinson defines a cynic:*** Kerry Alys Robinson serves as an Executive Partner of Leadership Roundtable, where she leads its work to expand globally and connect with Catholic leaders across the country and abroad. Kerry has been with Leadership Roundtable since its inception, serving as its founding Executive Director for 11 years, and its Global Ambassador for four years.